September 30, 2015

GRACE
IN A
WINTRY
SEASON

Feeling our Creator's love in a
world grown distant and cold
—and loving in return

Dr. Haight,

Thank you for your
fine works and
dedication

First Holy Communion, May 1950.

GRACE
IN A
WINTRY
SEASON

Feeling our Creator's love in a
world grown distant and cold
—and loving in return

Edwin Steinmann

FLORENCE FLEMING LLC

ISBN: 978-0-9961841-0-6
Library of Congress Control Number: 2015906364

Cover photograph: ©Elena Belozorova, Sunrise in the Winter, Thinkstock.com

Printed in the United States of America

[FLORENCE FLEMING LLC]

P.O. Box 365
Saint James, MO 65559

www.graceinawintryseason.com

To Elyse and Nathan,
with love and gratitude

If you want to understand human nature, the human mind, what makes us tick, you need to look at dreams.

—Patrick McNamara[1]

Carl Jung and other psychologists would encourage us to assign more importance to our dream life; it need not be a mere concession to some "primitive" instinct of human beings if God were also to use dreams as means for communicating revelation.

—Gerald O'Collins[2]

---

1. Patrick McNamara, PhD, interview excerpt, "What Are Dreams?" aired June 29, 2011, on NOVA, PBS, www.pbs.org/wgbh/nova/body/what-are-dreams.html.

2. Gerald O'Collins, SJ, *Rethinking Fundamental Theology* (New York: Oxford University Press, 2011), 77.

Contents

One
Christianity in Transition

I wanted to believe. I really did.

But I had doubts. Many of the things I had been taught growing up Catholic didn't make sense to me. For example, Jesus' rising up from the dead, walking around talking to people for forty days, then ascending into the sky and disappearing in a cloud. I found it hard to believe.

Not long ago, Pope Francis, whom I admire, said, "The most important thing is the first proclamation: Jesus Christ has saved you."[1] I was disappointed when I read this. I don't believe Jesus has saved us. It is what's projected onto Jesus, unwittingly, that saves us. It is our own inner death and resurrection, so to speak, that saves us.

I wish Francis, or his successor, would assemble the church's hierarchs and its women leaders and say something like this:

---

1. Antonio Spadaro, SJ, *A Big Heart Open to God: A Conversation with Pope Francis*, foreword by Matt Malone, SJ (published by the editors of *America*, 2013), Kindle edition, loc. 267 (chap. "The Church as Field Hospital").

Dear sisters and brothers, our beloved church is dying, especially in Europe and North America—as you well know. So many people are leaving, our young people in particular. If what I am told is true, we have lost our youth already. They don't attend mass and don't believe our teachings. If it is true that we have already lost them, how much time does our dear mother have left? Twenty years? Thirty?

We have many problems. The overarching one is our theology. For many, it lacks credibility. It is seen as ridiculous.

We are still teaching—it is *still* in our catechism—that all of history, all of the world's suffering, has resulted from a wrongful act committed by our original parents. What is wrong with us that we are still teaching that? It should have been discarded long ago. People see us as fools or knaves or both for clinging to a story they know is false. What are we to replace that story with?

Something like this, I think: Astrophysicists tell us that before the Big Bang there was no time, no space, and no thing, and then bang!, there was. Accordingly, should we not be teaching, unless evidence someday demonstrates otherwise, that the no-time/no-space/no-thing Mystery is God hirself—I spell that h-i-r-s-e-l-f, meaning himself-herself-itself; it is about time we stop referring to God as male, don't you think?—that God hirself incarnated and became, in part at least, the Universe, meaning that everything in the Universe is God in one form or another, that each of us is God in the form of an individual human being with all the limitations being human entails, and that all our suffering and the suffering of all other beings is actually God's suffering, is the price God has paid and is continuing to pay for incarnating. And that without such suffering, without hir self-sacrificing, we would not exist.

Should we not be focusing our attention on contemporary cosmologists as well as on ancient and medieval thinkers? And also on Jewish scholars? We tend to forget, don't we, that Jesus was Jewish, not Roman Catholic.

What should I, your pope, be doing? Many insist my job is to maintain the status quo. But is it, when the status quo is killing us?

What I am going to do is appoint a commission to re-examine the church's basic teachings. Fall/Redemption theology is going to be replaced with a theology that does justice to the grandeur of God's incarnation as the Universe and to hir continuing evolution as such—a theology of evolutionary incarnation.

I will direct the commission to reconsider the belief that gave rise to the church in the

first place—Jesus' resurrection from the dead.
Do we really understand what the apostles and
others saw when they experienced Jesus as
alive again, especially when we consider that
in biblical times people believed that God and
"his" angels appeared to them in dreams and
visions?

We need to consider whether the resurrection appearances were internal or external.
Have any of us seen a person who has been
dead three days come back to life, other than
in a dream or vision?

If it were *imagery* of Jesus alive again the
first Christians saw in dreams and visions, not
Jesus himself, has our faith been in vain? No,
but it has been misunderstood, misconceived.

I am going to direct the commission to consult not only with theologians, biblical scholars,
historians, and cosmologists but also with depth
psychologists, those psychologists having some
understanding of the psychological-spiritual
meaning of dreams and visions and the entity
creating them.

I know this is a big step, and many will
disapprove. But what other choice is there?
Without our young people to carry on, it's not
a matter of whether the church, our mother,
will expire but when—and the clock is ticking.

> Will you help me? Will you help me rebuild
> our crumbling church?
> Please pray for me, brothers and sisters, and
> for one another, and for our dear mother.

I know, you don't have to say it; Francis is not likely to say anything like this, nor will any successor in the foreseeable future. It is difficult to accept the idea that the church has misunderstood things since its beginning.

But some things have been misunderstood. I say that because I believe I have experienced a vision similar to what the first Jesus followers experienced. It was not a vision of Jesus alive again but of imagery of him alive again. It was beatific, both in its magnificence and effect. I understand the life-changing, belief-changing impact such a vision, or dream, would have had on the first Jesus-followers. It would have induced them to compose the hymn in Philippians 2:5–11:

> Let the same mind be in you that was in
> Christ Jesus,
>> who, though he was in the form of God,
>> did not regard equality with God
>> as something to be exploited,
> but emptied himself,
>> taking the form of a slave,
>> being born in human likeness.
> And being found in human form,
>> he humbled himself

and became obedient to the point
of death—
even death on a cross.
Therefore God also highly
exalted him
and gave him the name
that is above every name,
so that at the name of Jesus
every knee should bend,
in heaven and on earth and under
the earth,
and every tongue should confess
that Jesus Christ is Lord,
to the glory of God the Father.[2]

I cannot imagine myself a first-century, mono-
theistic Jew composing this hymn unless I had seen
an image of Jesus alive again that was so out of the
ordinary that it would have convinced me that he had
been a preexisting divine being of some kind who
had become human and was subsequently elevated
to an even higher status upon being raised up from
the dead by God "himself"—which is similar to how
the risen Christ figure in the vision I had struck me,

---

2. For a brief discussion of the Christ hymn, see *The Jewish Annotated New Testament*, eds. Amy-Jill Levine and Marc Zvi Brettler (New York: Oxford University Press, 2011), 357. See also Alan F. Segal, *Two Powers in Heaven* (Waco, Texas: Baylor University Press, 2012; Leiden: E.J. Brill, 1977).

a twentieth-century (at the time), German/Irish, North American cradle-Catholic, the huge difference being that I realized it wasn't Jesus alive again visiting me but rather an *image* of him alive again that I was seeing.

If Peter and the other apostles, including Paul, were somehow pulled out of the hereafter and given a contemporary education, one that included the best of depth psychology, would they still believe they saw Jesus alive again or would they now believe they saw imagery of Jesus alive again, imagery created by the same entity who creates dreams in them every night and visions sometimes also? It would be the latter, I think. I say "who creates" rather than "that creates" because the dream-vision creator, in my experience, has a personality; s/he (he-she-it) is not indifferent about our attitude toward hir.[3] The dream-vision creator sometimes images hirself as male, sometimes as female and sometimes neither.

Is a new image of Jesus slowly emerging, I wonder: Jesus the Projection-Carrier, the (subconscious) projection-carrier of our own inner death and resurrection, of our own human-divine oneness—an image supplanting those in past centuries?[4] Such is the image I now have of Jesus.

---

3. For comments regarding the issue of God's possessing a personality, see Carter Phipp's interview of John Haught at bigthink.com/the-evolution-of-enlightenment/a-theologian-of-renewal.

4. Jaroslav Pelikan, *Jesus Through the Centuries: His Place in the History of Culture* (New Haven: Yale University Press, 1985).

The story of the emergence in me of this new image of Jesus begins at a dinner party in 1984 with the hostess showing me a book she was reading, given to her by a nun-friend who loved it, John Sanford's *Healing and Wholeness.* Sanford, an Episcopal priest and Jungian psychoanalyst, maintained in effect that there is a Center in each of us that knows us better than we know ourselves, loves us more than we love ourselves, and is always trying to heal our woundedness through the dreams and visions it creates in us, and otherwise.

That was news to me. If it were true, if this Godlike Center really existed and is communicating "itself" to us lovingly in dreams and otherwise, what would that mean? That the universe is friendly? That it is not the indifferent machine it seemed to me to be? Given all the unmerited suffering in the world, human and otherwise, how could such possibly be true? It couldn't be.

My opinion of God at the time was negative. The negativity, which I suppressed, began in my twenties while working as a juvenile officer for the Circuit Court of the City of Saint Louis, Missouri. It was there that I saw for the first time the heartbreaking effects of poverty. I was in the investigation unit; we prepared certain cases for hearing—the homicides, nearly fatal assaults, rapes, and armed robberies.

Some of the cases still haunt me: the girl whose eyes were gouged out with a broken drinking glass so she couldn't identify her rapist; another girl shot dead in an alley, the word "pussy" written in her blood on a garage door; the neighborhood wino doused in gasoline and set on fire, just for the fun of watching him scream and die; the frightened little boy sitting in darkness not far from me—I was working the booking desk that night—dumped at the detention center by his aunt who didn't want him, his mother having died recently, his father long gone.

Where was God?

Following the dinner party, I ordered a copy of Sanford's book and read it quickly when it arrived. Impressed but skeptical, I put the book aside and forgot about it for a while. After all, if things were as Sanford said, my so-called education had missed the mark widely, and I considered that highly improbable.

Eventually, recalling some of the things he had written, I paid attention to a dream for the first time ever. The dream changed me. Two months later, I had the extraordinary inner vision. It changed me even more.

There is an aspect of life about which we are taught nothing. Our teachers and religious leaders can't teach what they don't know, of course; no one has taught them. Sanford was taught by a psychoanalyst, Fritz Kunkel,[5] who was strongly influenced by Carl Jung, the Swiss psychiatrist.

---

5. *Fritz Kunkel: Selected Writings,* edited, with an introduction and commentary by John A. Sanford (New York: Paulist Press, 1984).

What Sanford learned indirectly from Jung was to pay attention. Jung had turned inward after breaking off his relationship with Sigmund Freud, had analyzed his own dreams and visions and then shared what he had managed to comprehend. Of his initial turning inward, Jung wrote:

> When I had the vision of the flood [covering a part of Europe] in October of the year 1913, it happened at a time that was significant for me as a man. At that time, in the fortieth year of my life, I had achieved everything that I had wished for myself. I had achieved honor, power, wealth, knowledge, and every human happiness. Then my desire for increase of these trappings ceased, the desire ebbed from me and horror came over me. The vision of the flood seized me and I felt the spirit of the depths, but I did not understand him. Yet he drove me on with unbearable longing and I said:
>
> My soul, where are you? Do you hear me? I speak. I call you—are you there? I have returned, I am here again. . . . [One] thing you must know: the one thing I have learned is that one must live this life.
>
> This life is the way, the long sought-after way to the unfathomable, which we call the divine. . . . What words should I use to tell you on what twisted paths a good star has guided

me to you? Give me your hand, my almost forgotten soul. How warm the joy at seeing you
again, you long disavowed soul. Life has led
me back to you. Let us thank the life I have
lived for all the happy and all the sad hours, for
every joy, for every sadness. My soul, my journey should continue with you. I will wander
with you and ascend to my solitude.[6]

The grace of which I speak in this little memoir
is the love I have experienced in my journey, my pil-
gramage to the Mystery in the depths of my soul, and
the wintry season, today's pervasive disenchantment,
the result of faith's "melancholy, long, withdrawing
roar."

---

6. Carl Jung, *The Red Book*, intro. Sonu Shamdasani, eds.
Mark Kyburz, John Peck, and Sonu Shamdasani (New York:
W. W. Norton & Company, 2009), 232.

Two

But Now My Eye Sees You

October 1984

It is a beautiful fall evening. Elyse and I are on a brief vacation, staying overnight in the lodge at Roaring River State Park in southwest Missouri. John Sanford's book comes to mind, and I decide to find out for myself whether he knows what he is talking about. I'll pay attention to any dream I might have tonight and see whether it makes sense, whether it will have been worth the effort.

I am forty-two, a lawyer, and have never paid attention to a dream before. I know I have dreams, but I don't remember them. Elyse, my wife, is thirty-two and a nurse. She has never paid attention to her dreams either.

I want to be scientific, and so I form a null hypothesis before going to bed: If I have a dream tonight and remember it and write it down and analyse it, I will have wasted my time because, as everyone knows, dreams are nothing but garbage heaps of repressed desires having no spiritual meaning whatsoever. If there

13

is any evidence that dreams are spiritually meaningful, I will recognize it. I will see whether my education has been hugely deficient, has missed the mark.

Early the next morning, I lie in bed and realize I am dreaming. The dream seems absurd, but I remember having resolved to pay attention to any dream I might have and so force myself to do so. When the dream ends, I tiptoe through the dark room so as not to awaken Elyse, enter the bathroom, shut the door, turn on the light, sit on the floor, and record the dream on the pad of paper I had laid beside the bed the night before. I berate myself for being such a fool, wasting time with this nonsense when I could be in bed sleeping.

The dream:

But Now My Eye Sees You

Everyone in the huge, old courtroom is looking at me, the prosecutor, waiting for me to proceed. But I don't know what I am doing! How did I get into this?

I don't know what the case is about. I don't know who the witnesses are or what the other evidence is. I don't know anything! I feel like running out of the courtroom, but I'm not going to. I am going to see this through to the end no matter what.

I am standing at one of the two counsel tables. To my right, at the other counsel table, are the defendant and his lawyer. I am addressing the judge. The defend-

*ant's lawyer is also standing. He is objecting to what-
ever I am saying.*

*Seated to his right is the defendant. I look at him
briefly and turn away in disgust. He is a denizen of
the gutter—an old, irresponsible skid-row bum. His
crumpled, threadbare suit looks as if it has been worn
continuously for months. He needs a bath, a shave, a
haircut, and new clothes.*

*Every time I say something, the bum's lawyer objects,
and the judge sustains the objection. His lawyer is not
letting me get away with anything. The judge, a kindly,
gray-haired old man, is becoming impatient with me.*

There are only three jurors—three elderly men.

*Because I am confused and anxious, everyone else
is also—except the defendant. He is calm. He seems
oblivious to the proceedings.*

*The judge says something to me, and I respond. The
bum's lawyer objects, and the judge sustains the objection. I realize that I have nothing else to say; I have run
out of blarney. Something horrible is about to happen;
I can feel it. Maybe I'm going to have a heart attack or
lose my mind!*

*Just then, the bum, still seated, addresses the judge:
"All I ever wanted was twenty-five hundred dollars and
a little Schlitz."*

*Immediately the mood in the courtroom changes.
Everyone is now laughing and smiling, except me. I just
stand there, wondering what in the world is going on. I
feel better, though. The trial is over.*

The bum's lawyer removes a checkbook from his briefcase, writes a check for twenty-five hundred dollars, and hands it to the defendant. The defendant then hands him a rubber stamp and an inkpad. This is odd, I think. What is this? Then I realize that the rubber stamp and ink pad have something to do with the defendant's business, and that's what the trial has been about—the defendant's rubber stamp business. I don't get it. What does this mean? I just stand there.

While I'm looking at the bum, he turns and looks at me. His eyes are filled with love and joy. I feel both. He is pleased with me, pleased that I didn't run out of the courtroom, even though I felt like it. I realize that he is not a bum at all! He is extremely intelligent.

Gazing into his eyes, I realize that it was he who created this trial and put me in it and that he did so for my benefit. I don't understand. Nevertheless, I feel myself loving him in return!

I am fascinated. What is happening?

I am now walking north along Vandeventer Avenue near Saint Louis University, approaching a bar, the grand opening of which is being celebrated. The owners are my girlfriends, three beautiful women in their early twenties. They are standing in the doorway. When they see me, they wave and call to me to join them. I have to be elsewhere soon but say I will join them for a little while. They are pleased and say they won't keep me. I love them and am happy to be with them.

I step inside. There are a few tables, a bar, and bar stools. We sit at a round table in the center of the rectangular room. Several graduate and undergraduate students are laughing and having a good time. We are served a pitcher of beer. We talk awhile, laugh, and enjoy one another's company. I share their excitement and joy. When I finish a glass of beer, it is time for me to leave. I stand up and excuse myself.

I am now standing on the sidewalk in front of a one-story, rectangular building housing three different businesses. I am in front of the business in the center. It is the rubber stamp company the defendant sold to his lawyer.

I look to my left and observe the business there—a fruit and vegetable shop. Long tables are filled with fresh fruit and vegetables. I look to my right and see that the business there is an art and antique shop. Paintings are on the walls, and the shop is full of antique furniture and sculpture.

Inside the rubber stamp company is an old man who has worked there many years. He knows the business thoroughly. Next to him is the defendant's lawyer, the new owner of the business. Standing in the doorway in front of me is the lawyer's wife. She is feminine, intelligent, artistic, beautiful. She is examining the doorjamb, peeling away some cracked paint. She is pleased that her husband has acquired this business and the old building.

"I am going to strip away this old cracked paint and expose the natural wood underneath and turn this old building into a work of art," she says.

The old man asks the defendant's lawyer, "Can I stay on?" The lawyer responds, "You certainly can. I can't run this business without you."

I feel very good observing the old man, the lawyer, and his wife. I am filled with confidence and am ready to return to the courtroom, ready for the next trial, whatever it might concern.

"So this is what religion is *really* all about!" I said to myself shortly after recording the dream, feeling a tear rolling down my face, realizing my life had just changed.

What I understood was that religion was really about a relationship—the relationship between the two minds in my head, so to speak, between my conscious self and the mind who had just created the dream. It wasn't about dogmas and doctrines, as I had previously believed.

I realized that the trial in which I didn't know what I was doing was a metaphor for my life at the time. My life was a trial, an ordeal, one in which I didn't know what I was doing but nevertheless needed to proceed; bills had to be paid, and so on.

I understood too that because the defendant had created the trial, he was an image of the Creator of my life; he was an image of God, the God I had been putting on trial in my mind for many years, ever since working as a juvenile officer. That God was a shiftless bum, ultimately responsible—for all the world's unmerited suffering. The entity who had created the dream, though, wasn't like that; "he" was loving and joyful and wise, and I was loving in return!

While all this was sinking in, the last stanza of my favorite poem crossed my mind:

> Ah, love, let
> us be true
> To one another! for the world, which seems
> To lie before us like a land of dreams,
> So various, so beautiful, so new,
> Hath really neither joy, nor love, nor light,
> Nor certitude, nor peace, nor help for pain;
> And we are here as on a darkling plain
> Swept with confused alarms of struggle and
> flight,
> Where ignorant armies clash by night.[1]

Matthew Arnold had been wrong about life. All the things that he said were lacking in the world, weren't. I had just experienced them in the dream, and it was as real as anything else is real.

---

1. Matthew Arnold, "Dover Beach," in *Poetical Works of Matthew Arnold* (1890, 1891; Project Gutenberg, 2009), Kindle edition (no images), loc. 2752.

With the passing of time, I was able to understand other things—the rubber stamp imagery, for instance.

A few years before the dream, when I was an assistant prosecuting attorney in Cole County, Missouri, the local circuit clerk used a rubber stamp to authenticate copies of original documents—child support orders, for example. I would mail a stamped, authenticated copy of such an order to the prosecutor in the jurisdiction in which a defaulting parent resided—Los Angeles, for instance. The authenticated copy, stamped with the clerk's official seal, was as valid, as real, as the original order itself. The circuit clerk didn't have to travel to Los Angeles and testify that the copy was authentic; the authenticated, stamped copy was "self-authenticating."

In the dream, it was I who was being stamped and authenticated with my Creator's love and joy and wisdom. S/he, the dream-creator, was the original; I was a stamped copy made in hir image. S/he stamped hirself into me, so to speak, gave hirself to me using the image of the loving, joyful, wise "bum" to do so.

The grand opening of my girlfriends' business was another metaphor. It expressed the grand, the first opening of my mind to the dream-creating entity, the first time I paid attention to a dream. It was also grand in the sense of being hugely significant. The love and joy and wisdom that wasn't in me before the dream was there afterward.

Was Schlitz the beer served in my girlfriends' bar, the beer the defendant had said he wanted? Was the twenty-five hundred dollars the defendant had said he wanted a metaphor for the small amount of energy or effort it took to open up my mind to the dream-creator?

Were the three girlfriends a feminine trinity of sorts, another loving, joyful, wise God-image?

The last scene suggested to me a movement from left to right, from the fruit and vegetables on the left through the rubber stamp company in the middle to the works of art on the right—a movement from untransformed Nature through the authentication process to transformed Nature, the works of art. If so, what did that movement mean?

The defense attorney's wife said she intended to strip away the building's old cracked paint, expose the natural wood underneath, and turn the old building into a work of art. Was she talking about my old, worn-out persona, the Ed I had been showing the world and myself for years? Did she intend to strip old Ed away and bring to the fore my natural, authentic self?

Who was she anyway, and who was her husband, the defendant's lawyer?

A few days after the dream, the Book of Job came to mind, specifically Job's saying:

> I had heard of you by the hearing of the ear,
> but now my eye sees you;
> therefore I despise myself,
> and repent in dust and ashes. (Job 42:5, 6)

Job had asked for a response from God concerning his unmerited suffering and eventually received it in the form of a whirlwind, demonstrating God's incomprehensible, overwhelming power and intelligence. Job then saw, then understood, that God's ways were beyond his ability to comprehend, that he would never understand why God let innocent people suffer. He gave up his complaining, his putting God on trial.

The dream was for me something like the whirlwind was for Job. I ceased putting God on trial. My eye saw "him."

Three
Behold, We Know Not Anything

There were a few times when I convinced myself I did believe the things I had been taught. One of those times was during a retreat junior year in high school and for a while thereafter. I was seventeen.

I attended a three-day retreat because I was told there was a lake on the retreat grounds I could fish. I had no intention of praying or whatever one was supposed to do on a retreat. Religion didn't interest me; what interested me was chemistry, physics, and girls.

The retreat master, Brother Laurence, excelled at his job. Despite my lack of interest, he succeeded in getting me to think about spiritual matters. His guided meditations in the candlelit chapel took me back to the foot of the cross as Jesus hung dying. Although I had heard about Jesus' crucifixion countless times, it was during one of Brother Laurence's meditations that I, for the first time, became aware of the excruciating suffering involved. I was grateful for the suffering Jesus had endured on my behalf.

Brother Laurence also got me thinking about my future. In the weeks following the retreat, especially at night lying on the bench in the backyard, gazing at the stars, feeling as if they and I were closely connected fellow travelers in life's great adventure. Where in the scheme of things did I fit in? I wondered.

I eventually concluded that I wanted to give back to God the life "he" had given me; I would become a priest. Although I wanted to be a husband and father someday, I convinced myself that I could handle celibacy.

I applied for admission to the archdiocesan high school seminary, Saint Louis Preparatory Seminary. It was in Shrewsbury, the Saint Louis suburb in which we lived. It was within walking distance. That seminary doesn't exist today. Enrollment declined sharply in the sixties and thereafter. It has been a wintry season for faith.[1]

Following an interview with the pastor of our local church, my application was approved. I would spend my senior year, 1959–60, in the seminary instead of in the co-ed archdiocesan school I had been attending for three years, Bishop DuBourg High School.

Things changed over summer vacation, though. Early that summer, thinking I should acquire all the wisdom I could, since I would someday need it as a priest, I checked a philosophy book out of the county bookmobile when it was parked in Shrewsbury. What

---

1. Karl Rahner, *Faith in a Wintry Season: Conversations and Interviews with Karl Rahner in the Last Years of His Life*, eds. Paul Imhof and Hubert Biallowons, trans. Harvey D. Egan, SJ (New York: Crossroad Pub. Co., 1991).

I knew about philosophy was nothing other than it had something to do with wisdom.

I didn't get further in the book than an early section on Plato and Socrates. Socrates's teaching method fascinated me, the way he posed one seemingly simple question after another, leading his pupils inexorably to the shocking realization that what they really knew was nothing. I admired Socrates for his pursuit of truth and wanted to be like him; I wanted to follow truth wherever it would lead. I decided to start with myself. I would interrogate myself as Socrates had interrogated his fellow Athenians.

The self-examination went something like this: What if, Ed, everything you have been taught is wrong? What if the nuns and priests who have taught you have been well intentioned but mistaken? What if Jews or Protestants or Muslims or Hindus know what they are doing but not Catholics? How do you know God is good? Why do you call God "he"? Does God have a penis? If so, what does he do with it? Were there really an Adam and an Eve and a Fall? If not, why is there suffering and death? Is the pope really infallible? Who are you anyway, Ed? What are you?

Realizing everything I had been taught could be wrong, becoming a priest no longer made sense. I didn't enroll in the seminary in September but stayed at DuBourg.

During senior year, in a conversation with a priest at the school, I mentioned that I didn't believe the pope was infallible. He asked whether I had expressed my disbelief to anyone. I said that I had. He said that under canon law I had automatically excommunicated myself: One was permitted to think such a thought, that the pope was not infallible, but one was not permitted to publicly express it.

Nothing changed externally. I didn't have to wear a big scarlet X on my shirt or anything, but I nevertheless felt like an outcast ogre. After a couple of weeks, I convinced myself that I really did believe in papal infallibility in matters of faith and morals, just as I had been taught, and told the priest so. He was relieved and in my presence called the chancery and asked what needed to be done to lift the excommunication. Nothing, he was informed; my verbal recantation was sufficient. It felt good being a member of the flock again.

But the feeling didn't last. I soon realized I really didn't believe the church's teaching about infallibility. And I felt ashamed for having been so easily intimidated and manipulated. I didn't talk much to the priest after that. I didn't fully realize it then, but my Catholicism had ended.

From time to time, I remember this event and wonder how things would have played out had I attended the local Jesuit high school instead of the archdiocesan one and had mentioned my disbelief to one of the Jesuits there. Would he have congratulated me for possessing a functioning brain? Would I be a Jesuit now?

As the years passed, I disregarded religion. I couldn't relate to it.

I kept busy, attending school and working. I worked in a grocery store and attended Saint Louis University (SLU), a Jesuit institution, where my friends were enrolled. After sophomore year, I quit college, bored and confused and in need of funds. I worked a year as a materials inspector for the Missouri Highway Department, inspecting limestone aggregate and sand at various quarries and sand plants. The job allowed me to read at times, and I did.

I returned to SLU for my junior year but after one semester transferred to the University of Missouri–Columbia (Mizzou). It was time to move on, to leave home. After graduating from Mizzou with a B.A. in English Literature, I returned to Saint Louis and worked my way through SLU's School of Law.

Upon graduation I returned to the juvenile court, in the legal unit not the investigation unit. Thereafter I was a public defender, also in Saint Louis.

During this time, my father and I built, with some help from a retired carpenter, a cabin in the country about a hundred miles west of Saint Louis. I developed a love for the country, for the peacefulness. I wanted to move there, but as close to rural life as I could come was Jefferson City in the middle of Missouri. I took a job as legal counsel with the Division of Family Services, litigating, drafting legislation and rendering legal opinions to staff.

One day in the office a fellow attorney's daughter brought him lunch, and he introduced us. Elyse was striking in her white nurse's uniform, so very feminine, so beautiful. I asked her to lunch. We hit it off immediately. She had graduated from SLU also. Much later I learned that her father had orchestrated our meeting. He considered me son-in-law material after I had once mentioned that my favorite poem was *Dover Beach*. He had written his master's thesis on Matthew Arnold.

Both Elyse and I had had enough of the single life. We were ready for marriage and children.

When our son, Nathan, came into the world—he arrived via C-section—we were ecstatic. I saw him for the first time in the nursery. He was swaddled in a blue blanket, his tiny fingers touching his tiny ears, his eyes gazing at a light in the ceiling; I loved him immediately and deeply.

But there was a problem—not with him, with me. I wanted to give him a world filled with love and beauty and joy and fairness, but couldn't. I didn't know such a world.

What had gotten me through the years from my excommunication experience in 1959 to that first dream, *But Now My Eye Sees You,* in 1984 was not religion but an innate basic trust, the sort of thing Tennyson had written about:

Behold, we know not anything;
I can but trust that good shall fall

At last—far off—at last, to all,
And every winter change to spring.[2]

Shortly after Nathan was born, Elyse and I thought about joining a church, but neither of us could bring ourselves to do it. I had not forgotten the excommunication, and she had unpleasant memories of the Protestant church in which she had been raised. But when Nathan was six, figuring we had waited long enough, if not too long, we visited some local churches.

When we visited the Methodist church, we were immediately and strongly drawn to the pastor, the Reverend Gene Rooney. Whatever he said during his sermon, it hit home. It was as if he were speaking directly to us. Thereafter we attended church regularly. We looked forward to Sunday mornings. We very much wanted to believe. We suppressed our doubts and hoped some of pastor Rooney's faith and wisdom would eventually rub off on us.

I remember saying to him on the Sunday morning we officially joined, as we stood with him before the congregation, "I love this church." I meant it.

---

2. Alfred Lord Tennyson, *In Memoriam A.H.H. OBIIT MDCCCXXXIII 54* (1849, 1895; Poetry Foundation), http://www.poetryfoundation. org/poem/174608.

Four
Face to Face

December 17, 1984

The day began, two months after that first dream, *But Now My Eye Sees You*, with my driving sixty miles from Jefferson City to the Pettis County Courthouse in Sedalia, the site of the Missouri State Fair.

On the court's docket that day—for a trial setting, not for trial—was a case involving cattle that had been loaned to the Missouri Department of Agriculture, the entity that annually produced the fair. The plaintiff was a cattleman who had provided a hundred head for use in a roping exhibition, as I recall. I represented the department in my capacity as an assistant attorney general. The plaintiff maintained that ten head were missing when the cattle were returned to him and that fair employees had taken them. He wanted to be paid.

The department insisted that all of the cattle had been turned over to the truckers hired by the plaintiff for transport back to his ranch, and if ten head were missing, the truckers had taken them. The suit was an old one; it hadn't been pursued. It was on the docket that day because the judge, not the parties, had placed it there. The judge wanted the matter disposed of one way or another—by trial, settlement, or dismissal.

Several lawyers were present that morning handling uncontested divorces, arguing motions, and scheduling various matters. My missing cattle case was near the bottom of the docket and wasn't called up until late in the morning. All the while I sat there and stewed. I had other matters needing attention—tedious grain elevator insolvencies in particular.

As I waited, my mind wandered. I thought about time itself, about how limited and precious it was. I began reviewing my life, thinking about how much time I had thrown away on things that didn't matter. Eventually, the case was called and a trial date set. Driving home, I continued assessing my life, regretting the times I had frittered away, wondering what I ought to do with whatever time remained for me.

Back home, I was alone. Elyse was working, Nathan was in school, and Dorothy, Elyse's mother, who lived with us, was out with friends. I was miserable, feeling that I was squandering my life.

I grilled two cheese sandwiches and ate them while watching the goldfinches at the feeder outside the window next to the kitchen table. I envied the little birds. They weren't concerned about why they existed and what they ought to be doing with their lives; they were doing it. They were fully in sync with Nature.

What would it take for me, being human and not a bird, to be in sync with Nature, I wondered. Surely I would need to know who and what I was and why I existed, wouldn't I? But I didn't know.

That is when the thought occurred to me that maybe the dream-creator could communicate with me when I was awake as well as asleep. If s/he could, would s/he? What would happen, if anything, were I to put myself into a deep state of relaxation and ask hir for help? Probably nothing, I thought, but I decided to give it a try anyway.

Upstairs in a bedroom, I disconnected the phone; I didn't want to be disturbed. I lay in bed on my back, eyes closed, and cleared my mind as best I could, wanting to be as receptive as possible to any imagery the dream-creator might send. I put myself into a relaxed state using an exercise I had learned in an adult-ed stress-management class. I imagined a warm, heavy substance slowly moving from the tips of my toes to the top of my head. I imagined it many times.

I asked the dream-creator to send me any images that would help me understand who and what I was and why I was here, then paused and looked into the blackness behind my closed eyelids for any images that might appear. There were none.

"I knew this wouldn't work," I said to myself. But I didn't feel like giving up and repeated the exercise a few more times, continuing to look into the blackness. Then I stopped the exercise, and an image appeared!

Face to Face

A small white circle is in the center of the blackness! I realize the mind, the entity who had created But Now My Eye Sees You, *is responding to my plea for help. S/he is "talking" to me!*

For half a minute or so, there is only the one tiny white circle. It seems far away. Then, innumerable little white circles stream forth from the original circle, spinning, spiraling, and swirling symmetrically in all directions. I am astonished by the beauty of their movement. I am aware that I am not dreaming but am fully awake and aware also that what I am observing is an elaborate, intricate, joyful dance. The dream-vision creator is ecstatic. I feel hir joy!

The image of a child standing in front of our house in Jefferson City, celebrating the Fourth of July with Roman candles, crosses my mind. Is that child an image of me?

Eventually several circles emerging from the original tiny white circle form a white oval having a white circle in its center. It is an image of an eye.

I look at the eye for a long time, expecting it to do something, to change shape perhaps. But it doesn't. Confused and eventually growing a bit impatient, I say (internally, not out loud) to the dream-vision creator, "Why are you sending me a picture of an eyeball?"

Immediately the eye disappears, and a capital letter "I" takes its place. The dream-vision creator is announcing hir presence, identifying hirself, addressing me directly! I am bewildered and feel myself trembling slightly. I realize I am in a state of mind I know nothing about. I am fascinated.

I watch the "I" for some time, until it disappears. It is replaced by an image of a brown wooden crucifix on top of a dirt hill. I think of Calvary, the hill on which Jesus was crucified. Why this image?

Another image follows, the same cross but now a dying man hangs on it, his head slumped to his right. I cannot see his face distinctly but can feel his anguish. He feels abandoned, and so do I. What am I looking at? A visualization of the actual crucifixion of Jesus? How could that be? It can't.

I feel as if I am in both the past and present, as if there is only this very strange now.

Four white lines forming a horizontal rectangle, in the upper-right portion of the blackness, replace the image of the man dying on the cross. At first, I think it is just a rectangle and wonder what it has to do with the images preceding it, if anything. Then I realize it is an image of a coffin, the crucified man's coffin.

The coffin is now in the center of the blackness, and the crucified man is rising up from it, his

*hands on the sides of the coffin pushing himself
up. He is alive again! I can see, but not distinctly,
his smiling face. I feel his joy.*

*I now see this same man walking along a dirt
road toward me—the me observing the imagery
(I'm not in the image). The road runs diagonally
from the left background to the right foreground.
To the man's left are several green trees and
bushes. The area to his right is clear. He is wearing a tweed suit that resembles my best suit. His
shoes look like my best wingtips. There is dust on
them. I stay focused on the dust for a long time.*

*Midway along the dusty road, he stops and looks
directly at me—the observing me. We are face to
face. The thought occurs to me that the man I am
looking at is an extraordinary image of myself, but
I immediately dismiss the idea. This man is perfect
in every way—far beyond perfect, actually. He is
superhuman, he is divine. Obviously, this could not
be a picture of me.*

*I stare at his powerful shoulders and wonder
what I am looking at. It has to be an image of
immense strength and perfect health, I think.*

*I then focus on the man's chest. I can see
through his suit and shirt. In the center of his
chest is a glowing ball of light. I am amazed and
stay focused on the light, wondering what in the
world I am looking at. Eventually the word* vita
("veeta") pops into my mind, and I know at once

*that it is the Latin word for "life." I correct myself;
I am not looking at a picture of immense strength
and perfect health, I say to myself, but rather a
picture of Life!*

*I look at the man's face. I have never seen
anyone so happy. Just looking at him floods me
with joy. Whatever joy is, I am looking at a picture
of it. I stay focused on his face for a long time
and realize I have seen his eyes before. They are
the same loving, joyful, wise eyes of the defendant
in* But Now My Eye Sees You! *Are the defendant
and this risen man the same person? How could
that be? I don't understand.*

*The risen man then disappears. He is followed
by an image of a white oval against a black background. It is, I understand, an image of a vulva.
Why this image?*

*It is then replaced by an identical image with
a white cylindrical shaft, a phallus, penetrat-
ing it. I am surprised and wonder whether this
experience is going to turn into something por-
nographic. Why an image of sexual intercourse?*

*That image is replaced with another image, a
phallus. At the top left of the shaft are a few small
white dots arranged vertically. I understand them
to be images of spermatozoa.*

*The image of the white shaft gives way to that
of a large white circle containing a small white
circle in its upper-right area. I take the image*

to be that of a womb containing an embryo—a pregnancy resulting from the intercourse previously imaged.

The large circle reappears, now containing several smaller circles instead of one. The womb is fully pregnant.

A different circular image then appears, that of a planet. Earth? A patch of land resembling a continent occupies the top part of the planet. It is split in half, left and right. Water separates the two halves. An immense ocean covers the bottom of the planet.

On the land are seven babies, four on one half and three on the other. They have just been born, although they appear to be several months old. They are sitting up and looking all around. They are seeing the world for the first time and are amazed. I realize they were imaged previously as the small circles inside the large circle.

This imagery gives way to blackness with a tiny red ball in the center. It seems very far away, and it doesn't mean anything to me at first. It's just a little red ball, but then I realize that it is alive in some way I don't understand, and that it is full of power. I feel it is going to do something but don't know what. I wait, continuing to watch it.

Eventually, there is an extremely brief, barely discernible white flash. The red ball is gone. There is nothing but blackness. The tiny red ball must have silently exploded, I think. I wait for something to appear in the blackness. Nothing does. But I feel enveloped in a huge presence, as if I am inside the dream-vision creator's infinite mind. I feel that my little observing mind is actually hirs.

Although I see only blackness, I know this experience is not yet over. The dream-vision creator is still present; I feel hir.

A small white speck appears in the blackness. Then, slowly, another. Then another, and another, and so on. I don't understand what I am looking at but keep looking. Finally, I get it. "My God, I'm watching the Universe coming into being!" I say to myself.

I am keenly aware of the extraordinary state of mind I am in. It seems as if the dream-vision creator is Reality hirself, God, and is using my little mind, which is actually hirs, to observe hirself, to observe hir transformation from a tiny red ball billions of years ago into the Universe as s/he now exists—that s/he is both creating the imagery and observing it.

I feel that s/he has answered my plea for help, and it is time for hir to leave. But I don't want hir to leave, not yet! Not until I understand this experience.

Frantically, in an effort to comprehend, I run the various images through my mind, starting with the small white circle and ending with the

little white dots. It doesn't help. I don't understand.
I then run the images through my mind in reverse
order, thinking I might get a better perspective.
Again, it doesn't help.

Finally, I cry out (in my mind, not out loud)
"What are you trying to tell me?" I wait for a
response. There is none. There is only blackness
and silence.

Then, slowly and nearly inaudibly, a voice
whispers, "I — am — you."

Still trembling inside, the vision fades, and I
return to normal consciousness.

I remained in bed a few minutes wondering what I
had just experienced. I wanted to stay there but couldn't;
it was time to go to the office. I was not an efficient
employee that afternoon. So much energy was running
through me that it was difficult to concentrate. I had to
get up from my desk several times and walk around the
office.

I tried, without success, for a week or so to figure
out what sort of experience the inner vision had been,
then one day the term "mystical experience" crossed
my mind, and I knew at once that was what it had been
even though I didn't believe in such, in what the nuns
and priests had termed a "direct contact with God."

❖   ❖   ❖

I would like to go through the images at this point, one by one, giving you my current understanding of them, but if I did so you might think that I had quickly comprehended them; I didn't. So I will mention just a few thoughts now and return to the imagery later.

I think the tiny red ball represented the no-time/no-space/no-thing Mystery that astrophysicists speak of as preceding the Big Bang. I see it as a God-image, an image of Being hirself.

It disappeared in a flash of white light—light being a universal God-image. Was it the same white light that appeared in the chest of the risen Christ figure?

Since I will be discussing several dreams in addition to this vision, it will be helpful to have a name for the dream-vision creator. I am going to call hir *Vita*. S/he is, it seems to me, God in the form of the Universe, or "Mother Nature" or "Nature" if you prefer; s/he is the Universe functioning in and through our-hir three-pound human brain.

Many years after the vision, I came upon some statements Meister Eckhart, the 13th-14th century Dominican monk and mystic, made that reminded me of the vision:

I have a power in my soul which is ever receptive to God. I am as certain as that I am a man, that nothing is so close to me as God. God is closer to me than I am to myself: my being depends on God's being near me and

present to me. So He is also in a stone or a log
of wood, only they do not know it. . . . And I
am the more blessed, the more I realize this,
and I am the less blessed, the less I know this.[1]

Where creature stops, God begins to be.
Now all God wants of you is for you to go out
of yourself in the way of creatureliness and let
God be within you.[2]

Also, some things Saint Paul wrote that had never
made sense to me before the vision began to make
sense afterward. For example:

I have been crucified with Christ; and it is
no longer I who live, but it is Christ who lives
in me. (Galatians 2:19)[3]

1. Meister Eckhart, *The Complete Mystical Works of Meister Eckhart*,
   ed. and trans. Maurice O'Connell Walshe, foreword by Bernard
   McGinn (New York: Crossroad Pub. Co., 2009), 352.

2. Meister Eckhart, *The Complete Mystical Works of Meister Eckhart*,
   ed. and trans. Maurice O'Connell Walshe, foreword by Bernard
   McGinn (New York: Crossroad Pub. Co., 2009), 110.

3. Regarding such transformation, see Alan F. Segal, *Life after
   Death: A History of the Afterlife in Western Religion* (New York:
   Doubleday, 2004), 419; and, Alan F. Segal, *Paul the Convert: The
   Apostolate and Apostasy of Saul the Pharisee* (New Haven, CT:
   Yale University Press, 1990), 63.

Five
The Call

December 20, 1984 – January 28, 1985

In the days and weeks that followed the vision, I felt that the dream-vision creator wanted *everyone* to consciously relate to hir, and that I was being required to do something about it.

I couldn't shake that feeling, even though I considered it ludicrous. How could I possibly share the vision when I didn't understand it? Over the next month or so, I repeatedly objected to the obligation I was feeling. I didn't have the requisite knowledge. I wasn't a theologian or depth psychologist or neuroscientist.

One afternoon at the office, realizing the obligation I was feeling wasn't going to end, I took a short break and thought about the possibility of someday writing a book about the vision. A title immediately suggested itself: *The Nature of Reality*. That is what I felt I had encountered in the vision: Reality, God, Being hirself. I jotted down some subjects I thought necessary to cover: psychology, theology, Eastern and Western religion, philosophy, neurology, biochemistry, and so on.

I soon put the pen down, realizing I could never write such a magnum opus; I would never have the requisite knowledge; I would never be able to do justice to what *Vita* had given me in the vision.

That night I went to bed feeling that I was a failure, unable to carry the load that had been placed on my shoulders. The next morning, a dream:

The Call

January 29–31, 1985

Long ago, San Francisco Bay must have looked like this, I say to myself, standing on top of a hill overlooking a bay. There are no people, no buildings, no bridge. The sea is calm, the sky blue, the hills far across the bay, green. I feel the enormous power of the sea coursing through my body and am in awe of that power and of the beauty spread out before me. I am filled with a sense of adventure.

I walk down the hill toward the sea and see two wooden piers I had not noticed before. They are about a hundred yards apart, and each extends into the bay about a hundred yards. At the end of each pier, out over the water, is a wooden building. The buildings intrigue me, and I decide to investigate.

I walk along the shore to the first pier. The building at its end is small and square. I glance at the building at the end of the second pier and see that it is large and rectangular. It looks like a huge warehouse. I am curi-

ous about that building and walk along the shore over to the second pier and down that pier to the warehouse over the water. I stand next to it; it's to my left, the pier being L-shaped. As I stand there, again appreciating the beauty before me and feeling the strength of the sea, I hear the drone of a distant motorboat.

Looking across the bay, I don't see the boat anywhere and realize it must be to my left and obscured by the warehouse. The noise grows louder and louder, and I realize that the boat is speeding toward me. The boat is going to smash into the pier!

I start running down the pier toward the shore. When I'm close to the shore, the boat collides with the pier, and there is a terrific explosion! I turn around. The warehouse is gone! Tiny bits of debris are raining down from the sky into the bay.

I am afraid. Had I not moved, I very well may have been killed.

Looking at the end of the pier, now minus the warehouse, I catch a glimpse of a black speedboat, the boat that rammed the pilings under the pier and demolished the warehouse. It moves slowly toward the small square building at the end of the first pier. It strikes a piling beneath that pier and stops.

"Help me! Help me!" screams the man who was operating the boat. I can't see him; he's under the pier. He must be injured or drowning, I think. I want to help him but am afraid. He nearly killed me.

Looking in his direction, I remain on the second pier, wanting to help him but unable to move, my arms and legs paralyzed with fear. I feel horrible.

I wake up.

I am too upset to fall asleep again. I go downstairs to the kitchen table and reluctantly record the dream in my journal and then put it aside and get ready for work; I don't want to think about the dream. That day and the next, the paralyzed-with-fear dream ego (me in the dream) pops up in my mind several times. Each time I feel ashamed for not helping the screaming man, yet I don't want to deal with the dream; I want it to go away.

The third morning, I lie in bed, again remembering the dream. I feel that it is going to hound me forever unless I do something. The thought occurs to me that maybe it is possible to reenter a dream, and if so, maybe I could reenter this one and force the dream ego to swim over to the screaming man and help him—then maybe I wouldn't be bothered by this dream anymore. I decide to give it a try, even though I don't think it will work. I have never heard of reentering a dream, but what did I have to lose by trying?

I put myself into a relaxed state using the relaxation exercise I used before the vision and ask *Vita* to send the dream back to me. S/he does, immediately!

Everything is as before except there are now two of me: fully awake me observing the dream ("I"), and me in the dream, the dream ego ("Ed"). It is as if I am in an audience observing a play and at the same time an actor on stage performing.

Ed is still standing on the second pier near the shore, paralyzed with fear, looking toward the first pier. The man underneath the small building at the end of that pier is still crying out, "Help me!"

I want Ed to jump into the bay, swim over to the screaming man, and help him, but he doesn't. He doesn't move; he can't.

I realize that I have to do something to force Ed to move.

I imagine hitting him in his upper back as hard as I can with both fists. As I imagine it, I see Ed lurch forward, as if struck from behind (I do not see the fists). He teeters on the edge of the pier, nearly falling into the bay. I want him to fall in! But he doesn't. He straightens up and begins walking along the second pier toward shore and then along the shore toward the first pier!

Seeing this, I realize Vita *has taken over! That he should just walk over to the screaming man instead of swimming over to him had never occurred to either Ed or me. I am grateful and relieved that* Vita *has taken over. I have done, it seems to me, what s/he wanted me to do in reentering the dream and forcing Ed to move, and now s/he is going to resolve this drama. I feel that s/he is rewarding me and I can now lie back and watch the dream unfold.*

Walking along the first pier toward the small square building at its end, Ed stops for a moment and looks it over, then opens a door and walks in. There is only one room. It is dark. He has difficulty seeing but notices a trapdoor in the far left corner of the room. It has a heavy metal handle. He walks over to the trapdoor, pulls the handle, lifts off the door, and sets it aside.

Looking through the hole in the floor, he sees the black boat and catches a glimpse of the once-screaming man diving off the bow into the bay. The man's black trousers, black socks, and black shoes are all that Ed sees as the man enters the water. Immediately, Ed jumps through the hole in the floor of the building and onto the bow of the boat, then dives into the bay in pursuit.

In the water, Ed sees before him the man's trousers and shoes moving up and down as he descends at about a forty-five-degree angle. After a while, the man's clothes fall off. Continuing their long descent, the man eventually turns into a fish! Ed and I think this is extremely bizarre—a man turning into a fish!

Ed continues following the fish still deeper into the sea, and then Ed also turns into a fish!

Near the bottom of the sea, there is only blackness; light can't penetrate this deeply. Ed can no longer see the fish in front of him. Then, the fish begins glowing, and Ed can see it again. He continues following the fish. Eventually, to the left of the glowing fish, Ed sees a white, glowing ball of light on the bottom of the sea. It is small like a pearl.

Having seen the ball of light, Ed is no longer interested in the fish in front of him, and when it veers off to the right, he doesn't follow it but heads straight for the light on the bottom of the bay. When he reaches it, he opens his fish mouth and swallows it. He then turns upward and begins the long ascent to the surface, his fish body glowing in the darkness. Halfway up, he becomes a man again. His human body is glowing.

Reaching the surface, he is beside the black boat under the small square building at the end of the first pier. Pulling himself up onto the boat, he sees above him the square hole in the floor of the building and jumps up, grabs the edge of the floor, and pulls himself up and into the building. He walks through the dark room and out the front door, down the first pier toward shore, and then along the shore to the second pier where the big warehouse had been.

Standing on shore next to that pier and the debris-filled water, he is amazed at the devastation. There is nothing left of the warehouse except tiny particles. His body still glowing, he reaches over and touches the pier with his right hand. Immediately, the warehouse is perfectly reconstructed! There is no debris. Both Ed and I are astonished.

He walks over to the first pier and touches it. What-
ever damage had been done to that pier when the boat
struck one of its pilings is now repaired. Both Ed and I
feel the repair.

Ed then begins walking up the hill on the top of
which he was originally standing. Close to the top, he
pauses, turns around, and looks at the bay, again in
awe of its beauty and power. He feels close to the sea,
close to home. So do I. He turns and continues climbing
the hill.

The dream fades, and I feel wonderful, as if I have
been and continue to be in the presence of the divine.

❖   ❖   ❖

After the dream, still feeling the presence of the
divine, I lie in bed, amazed.

Later, I recorded the dream in my journal and realized that the man screaming for help didn't need any;
there was nothing wrong with him. "Help me!" was a
message he was delivering on behalf of the light at the
bottom of the sea. It was the light who wanted help,
not him. It wanted me to bring it up to the surface.

The large warehouse corresponded, I came to
understand, to the large book I had thought necessary
to do justice to the vision. Both were big containers,
the warehouse a container of items of one sort or
another and the book a container of information. In
demolishing the warehouse via hir messenger, *Vita*
was telling me to forget about the magnum opus.

What s/he wanted instead was for me to descend to the bottom of the sea, the sea representing the depths of my human soul, much of which is dark, that is, unseen by consciousness; hence, the term "the unconscious." One part of the unconscious is personal, that is, aspects of our personal experience in the world; and the other part is instinctual, inherited, universal, archetypal.[1]

The light in the blackness at the bottom of the sea, a God-image, wanted to be swallowed and brought up to the surface, to consciousness, to become conscious in me. S/he wanted to incarnate, to be embodied.

S/he, *Vita*, wanted me to reconstruct the warehouse, that is, to write the book *s/he* wanted, after I had descended the depths and brought hir up, not write the magnum opus, the big warehouse filed with ideas, the book I had thought necessary to do justice to the vision, *Face to Face*. As I came to understand the dream, *Vita* would be the book's content provider and I the ink pen.

But how was I to do that, to descend to the depths and bring *Vita* up?

By paying attention, it seemed to me, to the dreams s/he would henceforth create in me and by continuing

---

1. For levels of the unconscious and more, see C. G. Jung, *Memories, Dreams, Reflections*, Aniela Jaffe, ed., Richard and Clara Winston, trans. (New York: Vintage Books, 1989), 160; and, Murray Stein, *Jung's Map of the Soul, An Introduction* (Chicago: Open Court Publishing Co., 2001).

to ponder the meaning of this dream and that of *Face to Face* and *But Now My Eye Sees You.*

Years later, I read something Abraham Lincoln said and immediately thought of this dream:

> It seems strange how much there is in the Bible about dreams. There are, I think, some sixteen chapters in the Old Testament and four or five in the New in which dreams are mentioned. . . . If we believe the Bible, we must accept the fact that, in the old days, God and his angels came to men in their sleep and made themselves known in dreams. Nowadays dreams are regarded as very foolish, and are seldom told, except by old women and by young men and maidens in love. . . . After [a particular dream] occurred, the first time I opened the Bible, strange as it may appear, it was at the twenty-eighth chapter of Genesis, which related the wonderful dream Jacob had. I turned to other passages, and seemed to encounter a dream or a vision wherever I looked. I kept on turning the leaves of the old book, and everywhere my eye fell upon passages recording matters strangely in keeping with my own thoughts,—supernatural visitations, dreams, visions, etc.[2]

---

2. Ward Hill Lamon, *Recollections of Abraham Lincoln* (1895, 1911; Project Gutenberg, 2012), Kindle edition (with images), chap. VII, loc. 1707.

I have to ask: In this dream, did God and one of hir angels visit me in my sleep and make themselves known?

Does this dream belong to me alone? Or does *Vita* want each of us, to the extent we are able, to bring hir from the bottom of the sea to the surface?

Six
Paradise Lost

July 1, 1985

During the five months following *The Call* I paid close attention to every dream I could remember, recording each of them in my journal and analyzing them as best I could, trying hard to bring *Vita* up from the depths to the surface.

There was one dream, however, I refused to record. In it the dream ego was portrayed as a jerk of some sort, and I felt insulted and betrayed: I had been doing what I believed *Vita* had wanted me to do, and what I got in return was a dream that denigrated me. I was furious.

I told *Vita* to get out of my life and go screw hirself. I wasn't going to pay attention to hir anymore; s/he could cram hir bizarre dreams up hir ass and go straight to hell. I was going to do what I wanted to do when I wanted to do it, and the hell with hir.

The next morning:

Paradise Lost

A woman, a psychologist in her late thirties or early forties, theologically sophisticated, wise, feminine, attractive, and I are in a motel room, lying in bed, dressed, laughing at each other's jokes. I have known her only a short time but am fascinated by her and falling in love with her.

The door to the room opens and in walks the most beautiful woman I have ever seen. She is about twenty years old and has shoulder-length blond hair, blue eyes, and an angelic face. I am immediately attracted to her sexually. She smiles at me. She then unbuttons her blouse, revealing perfectly formed breasts. "I want you to make love to me," she says to me. I am beside myself with desire.

I look at the woman in bed with me, expecting her to be displeased. She isn't. She tells me to invite the young woman to join us in bed; she wants me to make love to her. I can hardly believe my good fortune.

The psychologist and I are now in Forest Park in Saint Louis, walking along a secluded path, enjoying each other's company, again telling jokes and laughing. We pause, and I lean toward her to kiss her, but she pulls back. I am disappointed and ask her why she didn't want me to kiss her.

"I'm married," she says.

I'm shocked. I had no idea she was married and am deeply hurt. She says her husband will be finishing his residency soon and starting his medical practice. It is obvious she loves him and is committed to him. I wish I were he. I want to spend the rest of my life with her.

I take a couple of steps along the path and turn to speak to her, but she isn't there. She has disappeared. I stand there, confused and hurt. After a while, I continue along the path and eventually stop at a refreshment stand.

Across the path from the stand is a large circus wagon and inside it, behind bars, is a wolf unlike any I have ever seen. He is gigantic. He is standing on his hind legs with his front paws high up on the bars. As soon as I see his eyes, I realize I am looking at evil itself, at the devil himself, Satan! His eyes are glazed and vacuous. He is completely insane. He is also vicious. I am afraid.

Instantly, he is out of the cage and on my back! My trousers are down, and he is ramming his immense penis up my rectum. The pain is unbearable. His penis is ripping my sphincter muscles to pieces. Blood is streaming down my legs. I cannot move. I cannot get away from him. Tears are streaming down my face.

I am now in a motel. The two women are there also. I'm in the bathroom bent over the washbasin, bleeding, applying a sanitary napkin to my anus. The pain is nearly unbearable.

Both of the women are in bed, waiting for me to join them. I see them through the open bathroom door. I very much want to be with them but can't move because of the pain.

The dream ends, and I awake extremely frustrated, confused, and in pain.

❖   ❖   ❖

It wasn't a good idea to tell *Vita* to go screw hirself and go to hell.

The jerk in the dream that I refused to deal with, I realized later, was a "shadow figure," an image of an unwanted part of myself, a part that *Vita* was calling my attention to and wanted me to face. I should have.

The wolf was an image of my self-destructive, wholly inappropriate, wrongheaded defiance, an attitude John Milton portrayed, in *Paradise Lost*, as Satan and expressed by his saying: "Better to reign in Hell than serve in Heaven."

In hell is where I ended up in the dream—completely frustrated, in pain, unable to unite with the women. Its opposite, heaven, would have been my being in bed with both women, having all of my needs and desires, spiritual and physical, fulfilled.

How many people, do you think, are reigning in hell and don't understand why?

Seven
The Boy in the Coffin

The Boy in the Coffin
September 6, 1985

*T*wo *brothers about ten years old are standing on a riverbank holding their bicycles, talking to their father. They ask if they can ride their bikes along the bank, and he says yes, so long as they are careful. They say they will be and ride away. Their father watches them ride off.*

The river bends to the right after a while, and the boys follow the bend. Eventually they come upon two coffins on the bank, one small and the other large. The boys slowly approach the coffins. The small coffin emits a foul odor.

At this point, I am awakened by Molly's yelping. Elyse had accidentally kicked our little terrier while walking through the bedroom. I go downstairs to the kitchen table, taking my dream journal with me, curious about the small coffin, wanting to know how the dream would have played out had I remained sleeping. Sitting at the kitchen table, eyes closed, I put myself into a relaxed state and watch what eventually appears in my imagination.

The two brothers are standing on the riverbank by the coffins. They hear a young boy in the small coffin screaming.

"Let me out of here! Let me out of this box!"

The brothers (whom I'll name "Yea" and "Nay") *are frightened and confused.*

Yea: "Let's open the coffin and let him out."

Nay: "No! He is rotten. He will infect us. He is evil. He will hurt us. He will kill us."

Yea: "No, he won't. He just wants to live. We can pull the coffin over to the river and pop the lid off and roll it over so he will be washed in the river. We won't have to touch him."

Nay: "Just getting near him will make us sick. The coffin is full of diseases. I don't want any part of this. I'm not going to help you. I'm leaving."

Nay gets on his bike and rides away toward their father. Yea watches him leave. It hurts him that his brother won't help him. He turns to the small coffin and says to the boy inside, "I am afraid of you. Will you hurt me if I let you out?"

Boy-in-coffin: "Just a little. But you can wash off in the river. If you help me, you will be far stronger than you will ever be if you don't let me out of here."

Yea: "Who are you?"

Boy-in-coffin: "I am a murdered child, but I'm not completely dead yet."

Yea: "How did you get here?"

Boy-in-coffin: "They buried me in the ground, but an underground stream came by and moved me over to this river. Then the river swept me to this place. I need you to open this box and let me out of here so I can live again."

While this conversation is taking place, I see a small coffin being lowered into a grave. A boy is inside the coffin, looking up through it and seeing several adults standing above him. He cannot see them clearly and doesn't recognize them. An underground stream then flows toward the coffin, causing it to move toward a river. The little coffin then floats away in the river and washes up on a riverbank.

Yea: "I am afraid you will hurt me, that you will put me in that coffin with you."

Boy-in-coffin: "I can't put you into this box. I don't have the power. I can't open it or close it."

Yea: "Why is that large casket here?"

Boy-in-coffin: "It's for you when you grow up if you don't let me out of here."

Yea: "Will you put me in it?"

Boy-in-coffin: "No. You will put yourself in it."

Yea: "I know somehow you are telling the truth. I will let you out."

Yea then notices a crowbar lying on the ground near the small coffin. He picks it up. Holding it in his *right hand, he grabs the handle on the front of the small coffin with his left hand and, walking backward, drags the coffin across the riverbank and into the river. He pries the coffin open with the crowbar. The top of the coffin falls into the river and is swept away.*

An offensive odor emanates from the coffin, so strong it causes Yea to fall backward into the river. Still holding the coffin, he looks inside and is surprised not to see the boy but only a few bones and pieces of decomposed black flesh. The coffin then tips over. The bones and rotten flesh spill into the river and are swept away by the current along with the coffin.

Yea pulls himself up and stands waist-deep in the water. His body is glowing.

Seeing this, I think some sort of spirit or energy, a light of some sort, must have exited the coffin and entered Yea and is now illuminating him.

He stands in the river awhile, watching the coffin float away, and then walks onto the bank. He is happy that he didn't ignore the screaming boy.

He gets on his bike and begins riding back to his father, his body continuing to glow.

I come out of my relaxed state, again amazed by what *Vita* has produced.

❖   ❖   ❖

When I was about four years old and following my mother down the basement steps to do the laundry, she turned and screamed at me, "I wish you had never been born!" It felt as if a big, rusty knife had been slammed into my heart. I just stood there.

I have come to understand that this dream was rooted in that incident and the effect the incident had on me. My mother's words played a role in my becoming a shy, quiet, insecure child, a child whose existence was a regretted mistake—a "murdered" little boy in a coffin.

Mother's name was Florence, but she was called "Rip." She was tough. She had issues. When she was in the eighth grade, the nuns came to the house and pleaded with her father to send her to high school. They said she was very bright and needed to go on in school, but her father refused, saying there wasn't enough money. Had she received an education, I doubt she would have been so frustrated and angry.

In midlife, she came down with lupus and also had a stroke. She suffered horribly for many years. In a hospital in her seventies, a few years after this dream, in a weak, distorted voice, she struggled to tell me how she had watched my sister raise her two boys with a lot of affection and how, seeing that, she realized that was how she should have raised us (Jane and Gene, my younger siblings, and me). Tears flowing from her legally blind eyes, she said she had done the best she knew how, raising us as she had been raised. That's when I forgave her for having "murdered" me.

She was lucky she had Dad to look after her during her thirty-year illness. He took good care of her. Tem-

peramentally, he was her opposite, gentle and kind.
But emotionally, he was distant. That's how he had
been raised. The only time I remember seeing him
angry was when we argued over my desire to attend
college. I was a senior in high school at the time. He
said that when the school year ended, I would need
to leave the house and be on my own, maybe join
the army. I said no, I was living at home and going to
college.

The matter was resolved, thanks to Mother's inter-
vention. I could continue living at home but would
have to pay for college myself.

Contemplating the dead boy in the coffin, I recalled
John Sanford's advice in *Healing and Wholeness* to
dialogue with the figures in one's dreams. Sanford said
that giving them a voice could sometimes uncover
their meaning and help in healing one's woundedness.
I decided to give it a try. I would dialogue with the
dead boy and see what would happen, if anything.

I dialogued with him many times, usually while at
the country cabin that Dad and I had built. I would put
myself in a relaxed state, and on the left side of a piece
of paper, I would write questions for him, and on the
right side, what I felt were his responses. I let little Ed
vent. There were no neighbors to hear the sobbing.

After a while I realized that the dialoguing was an
instance of the stripping away of the old paint the
defense attorney's wife in *But Now My Eye Sees You*

said she intended to do. She was busy stripping away dead Ed.

In *Face to Face* there had also been a coffin and a release therefrom—the crucified man's rising up from the dead. There was also light in *Face to Face*—the light in the risen Christ-figure's chest and the flash of light when the little red ball disappeared.

And in *The Call* there was the light at the bottom of the bay whose message, delivered by the screaming man, was "Help me!" *Vita* wanted to be brought up to the surface, to become conscious, to incarnate.

Whose life is each of us living?

Eight
Metanoia

Metanoia
September 29, 1985

*E*lyse and I are guests at a party in a mansion in Ladue, an affluent Saint Louis suburb. The home-owner and host is a lawyer I once met. I admire him because of the altruistic way he handled a lawsuit involving health club memberships. He could have accepted a settlement and taken a large fee for himself, but instead took the case to trial in an attempt to establish a precedent beneficial to health club members generally. His efforts were successful.

In the center of the mansion are an atrium, a waterfall, a pool of water, a large tree, a rock garden, and some green plants. Elyse and I are standing in this area, talking to a middle-aged, sophisticated, attractive woman who is a teacher and author. She is in excep-tionally good shape physically. She works out a lot, she says.

Seated on the floor near us is an archaeologist, a scholarly woman in her late sixties. A few people are also seated on the floor listening to her talk. We join the group. She is holding an ancient Greek manuscript she had recently excavated. It contains important material but is difficult to translate.

There is a heading on the manuscript consisting of three words. My eyes focus on the middle word: μετανοια. I see the letters clearly but don't know their English equivalents. I have no idea what the word means. The archaeologist says there is a large reward for whoever can correctly translate the manuscript.

The teacher-author is seated next to us. The archaeologist suggests to her that she should attempt to translate the manuscript, that she might be able to do it. She smiles and says that she may give it a try someday, but she's doubtful she can translate it.

Later in the evening, we are again talking to the teacher-author. She says she needs to leave and meet her daughter, that every week they get together and do something. She tells us what they have planned for the evening. (I can't remember what.) She mentions that the outing won't be expensive, only about sixty-nine dollars. As she leaves, Elyse and I say good-bye. We don't think sixty-nine dollars is inexpensive.

We are now standing on the sidewalk in front of the mansion. Someone walks by and asks where the host is. I reply that we don't know. I then look down the street and see an old red pickup moving slowly in our direction. It passes us, and I notice that our host is driving it. He is smiling, obviously enjoying the old truck. He prefers it to a luxury vehicle. Although he is affluent, he is not materialistic. He is spiritually rich.

The dream ends, and I awake feeling good.

❖   ❖   ❖

Seventeen years before this dream I thought that if I could read the New Testament in Greek, I could understand it. I was in the first semester of my last year of law school. I asked the Jesuit who taught the introductory Greek course in the College of Arts and Sciences at SLU, Fr. Haworth, whether I could sit in on his class. He said sure but on the condition that I participate in class along with everyone else. I agreed.

I enjoyed the class and wanted to take the second semester but couldn't because of a scheduling conflict. By the time of this dream I had forgotten whatever Greek I had learned years earlier. I had no idea what μετανοια meant.

A few days following the dream, I drove from our home in Jefferson City to my parents' home in Shrewsbury and retrieved from their basement the Greek dictionary I had used in Fr. Haworth's class. After much fumbling, I came upon μετανοια.

It means "afterthought" and is transliterated "metanoia." That didn't help much. Later I realized that the term was used in the New Testament and was translated as "repentance"—meaning a life-altering change in one's attitude, in one's heart and mind.

Although I had forgotten the meaning of μετανοια, *Vita* had not. S/he had used it in the dream because of a significant change of attitude occurring in me at the time. That change was the dialoguing with little Ed and its effect on me. I was releasing the boy instead of repressing him; I was enabling him to live, finally.

The mansion symbolized my soul, I think; and the tree, the Tree of Life, *Vita*; and the pool of water, that out of which we emerged long ago.

But the large reward the archaeologist spoke of— what was that about?

Nine
Abba

Abba

November 11, 1985

Lost, alone, and afraid, I am an orphan about four years old, standing in a clearing in a forest. A minister and his wife enter the clearing, take my hands, and lead me to their home. It is a simple log cabin in a primitive frontier area.

The cabin consists of one large room, plus bedrooms. The large room serves as a kitchen, dining room, and living room. There is a large, rectangular wooden table and a cast-iron stove. Behind the house are a barn and a corral.

The minister and his wife have adopted me. They love me as much as their three or four other children.

There is no affluence in this area, no money to build a church. Our log house functions as the church. Services consist of church members gathering around the table, my father giving a short sermon, and our sharing a meal. There is no falseness, no bickering.

Several years pass. Our small congregation endures many hardships—sickness, floods, drought. Whenever

71

difficulties arise, it is my wise and loving father who is sought and who holds our community together. He always knows what needs to be done and how to do it, how to comfort people when they are suffering. Everyone loves my father and trusts him. I am happy and content growing up in this home. I appreciate having been adopted into this family and am in awe of my father.

When I am in my early teens, one of my brothers is about eighteen years old. He tells Dad that he wants to play professional football. Dad is not enthusiastic. He tells my brother that by the time he is thirty, he may not be able to walk because of knee injuries. He says it would be smarter to start out with a part-time job that could turn into a career, maybe something in the life insurance business.

More time passes. When I am eighteen or so and alone at home, I realize there's an intruder in the corral behind the house. He has a weapon in his hand, a club. I know he has to be disarmed and driven off or he will kill someone. I am afraid of him. I don't want anything to do with this situation, but I have to deal with it.

I muster up the courage to walk to the corral but don't see the intruder. I soon find him in the barn. He still has the club. He is bigger and stronger than I am and vicious. I see it in his eyes. I am afraid. He starts walking slowly toward me, intending to use the club on me. I somehow manage to strike the first blow, and he goes down. He doesn't get up for a long time. When he does, he walks out the door and leaves. I am amazed I was able to stand up to him and drive him off.

More time passes. I am in my early twenties and a university extension agent of some sort. I marry my beautiful sister. Since we are not blood kin, it is okay.

A few more years pass. The members of our church community and my family are seated around the large table in our house. It is time for the sermon. My father sits to my right. He leans toward me and whispers that it is time for him to retire and for me to take over his ministry. He says I should give the sermon.

His retiring is news to me. I don't want him to retire! It would mean the end of our way of life, the end of the way things have always been. I don't want things to change, ever. Who would hold the people together if my father retired? Who would be wise enough? Certainly not me. I don't have his wisdom or strength. I don't want to be the minister!

He whispers again that I need to give the sermon, that the time has come for me to take over. He says there is nothing to worry about; everything will be fine. I don't want to give the sermon! I remain seated, hoping somehow to get out of this. But I can't get out of it. I stand up.

I say a few words and sit down. Much to my surprise, whatever I said, everyone liked it. They are pleased that I am their new minister. I am relieved. My father was right: The sermon was okay; I will be able to handle this responsibility.

*I sit there feeling the deepest and most complete joy
I have ever felt. My father is proud of me. I see it in his
loving, joyful, wise eyes.*

The dream fades away, and I awake feeling better
than I have ever felt—paradisiacally blissful, completely at peace, completely fulfilled.

❖   ❖   ❖

The never-felt-before paradisiacal bliss—was it the
large reward that the archeologist mentioned in *Metanoia* for correctly translating the difficult manuscript?

Was the manuscript the "script" I came into the
world with in need of translation, actualization?

As I understand the dream, *Vita*, imaged as my
wise and loving father, was the one who had taken
care of me all my life, had preserved little Ed in the coffin until he could be released. That time had arrived.
I was now assuming that responsibility, assuming
Vita's role, hir ministry. I was now nurturing dead Ed
back to life.

In *But Now My Eye Sees You*, the defendant's lawyer took over the defendant's business, the rubber
stamp company, the business of authenticating copies
of original documents. I was the copy being authenticated in that dream. In this dream, I took over my
father's business, his ministry—the equivalent of the
defendant's lawyer taking over the defendant's rubber
stamp company. In continuing to dialogue with dead
Ed, in authenticating myself, was I now functioning

as the defendant's lawyer functioned when assuming responsibility for the rubber stamp company, the authentication process?

Had I, in assuming my father's ministry, become in effect the defendant's lawyer?

Was my loving minister-father the equivalent of the loving, wise, God-image defendant?

In that first dream, the defendant's lawyer was married to a wonderful woman. In this dream, I was married to my wonderful sister. Taking both women as *Vita*'s way of imaging my closeness to hir, was I much closer to hir now than at first, since I was now *consciously helping hir* strip away the old, cracked paint, my old, worn out persona, thereby exposing my natural, authentic self, the script I came into the world with?

Was I now married to *Vita*? Is that what s/he was telling me?

Had *But Now My Eye Sees You* been a preview of coming attractions of sorts?

Did Jesus, who reportedly said that he must be about his Father's business, have dreams similar to this one?

Ten
The Women by the Pool
The Woman from Outer Space

March 1987

While on the road to Kirksville, driving through the rolling hills of northeast Missouri, the pastoral scenes along the way seemed like pictures in a coffee-table book rather than what they actually were, rural landscapes teeming with life. I felt sad and disconnected, as if something in me was dying.

There was a court hearing the next morning, another lawsuit involving cattle, not missing this time but infected with brucellosis.

In a motel in Kirksville, I tried dialoguing with the sadness, asking it to identify itself, to tell me what was wrong, but nothing came forth. In the days following, the sadness lingered. I tried repeatedly to understand it but couldn't.

Then one morning, a dream:

The Women by the Pool
March 21, 1987, 3 a.m.
I am walking along West Pine Boulevard a few

blocks west of Saint Louis University, carrying a suit-case, approaching a tall, modern, cylindrical apart-ment building. The Authority who decides where people live has determined that I am to live in this building. I am excited about moving in.

As I enter the lobby, an attractive, middle-aged woman greets me. She seems knowledgeable and in a position of authority. I tell her that I am here to move into the building and that my apartment number is 325 (or 345; I'm not sure). She tells me to follow her. We cross the lobby and enter an elevator.

The elevator rises and opens on the top floor. The floor is large and circular. In the center is a swimming pool. As we exit the elevator, I notice women in and around the pool. No men are present. I might be the only man in this building. What a wonderful thought that is! I would love to be the only guy here.

I notice a woman wearing a string bikini lying beside the pool. She has the most beautiful tush I have ever seen; I want to go over to her and squeeze it. I want to make love to her.

The woman guiding me and I walk along the cir-cular floor, passing one apartment door after another. They all open to this central swimming pool area. An attractive, intelligent-looking woman in a bathing suit is walking in front of us. As she opens the door to her apartment, she turns toward me and smiles. She is strongly attracted to me, I can tell, and I to her.

The women fascinate me. I want to make love to all of them. I can hardly wait to settle in and start meeting them.

As my guide and I walk farther along, things change.

We are now in an area that looks like an open hospital ward. There are hospital beds to our right instead of apartment units. Men occupy these beds; they look like they are dying. This area must be some sort of facility for the terminally ill, I think. I am afraid. Have I come here to die? I don't want to die! I want to live and make love to the women!

In the center of this area, instead of a swimming pool, there are small hospital beds for children. Dying boys, some of them babies, occupy these beds. They are pooping. I am frightened.

I tell the woman guiding me that some mistake must have been made. I don't belong here with these dying men and boys but over on the other side with the women. She says that she will go and see if a mistake has been made. She walks away in the direction of the elevator.

As she leaves, I am standing near the terminally ill babies. I feel horrible. I don't want to die!

I look at the dying babies and notice one in particular. He reminds me of a failure-to-thrive baby boy I once saw in a children's hospital. He was a few months old but wasn't developing. One of the nurses said that

his mother had rejected him and that he in turn was
rejecting life. I had felt sorry for him.

I am now feeling sorry for myself. I feel the residence-
determining Authority has decreed that I am to die here,
unfulfilled, never to be with the women.

I wake up, miserable, wondering what *Vita* has
just told me. Do I have to die before I can unite with
the women? I think that's it, but what sense does that
make? Nevertheless, I say to myself and *Vita*: "Well, if I
have to die to be with the women, so be it; let me die."

Three hours later, there's a second dream:

The Woman from Outer Space
March 21, 1987, 6 a.m.

I am in a large, high-ceilinged room in an immense
building, my place of employment. I am standing at a
workbench, doing my job, taking a box off a high shelf
on the wall in front of me, opening it and removing the
contents.

Time passes. Two men in the building have just
been murdered, I'm told. This frightens me. I am also
curious. I want to know what is happening but con-
tinue working.

More time passes, and I am now in the basement. It
is a huge and mostly open space. Standing in the center
some distance from me is my boss, the superintendent.
When he sees me, he motions for me to come over to him.

When I am next to him, he says, reaching down into a coffin-shaped hole in the concrete floor, "Look at this." He pulls up the corpse of one of the recently murdered men. The dead man is dressed in trousers and a white shirt and tie. The corpse is in an upright, sitting position. The top of his head is missing. It has been skillfully sawed off. I look into the cranium and see that it is empty. The murderer has removed the dead man's brain and eaten it, I think. I am scared. What kind of monster would do this, would kill a man and eat his brain?

I look again into the brainless skull and see a small object in its center that I had not noticed earlier. It is a vertical white shaft with thin, red, ribbon-like pieces outstretched on top. It looks something like an apple core with strips of red peeling extending outward from the core. It is somewhat umbrella-shaped but also phallic. The shaft then bulges out a little, and the red, apple-like strips disappear. It is now oval shaped and resembles a vulva. The object changes again and becomes round-ish and womblike.

I look up and notice in the distance and to my left a woman, dressed in black, head to toe, walking rapidly. On her head is something resembling a welder's helmet, a mask of some sort. I see changing red numbers through the dark eye windows.

The woman sees me watching her and quickens her pace. She exits the basement through a door to my right.

I tell the super about her and say, "The red numbers must be a part of the mask."

"No," he says, "they are not a part of the mask." I understand him to mean that the red numbers are actually her eyes! How can this be?

I want to know more about her and run after her. I think she must be the murderer. I want to know who she is and why she has killed the men and eaten their brains.

I am now alone with her in another room. We are facing each other. I know that she is not of this world, that she is from outer space.

"It's you, isn't it?" I say to her, meaning the killer.

"Yes," she says.

"Take off your mask," I tell her.

"No," she says.

"Why not?" I ask.

"Because you wouldn't like what you'd see."

"Take it off!" I insist.

Slowly, using her left hand, she pulls off the mask and tosses it to the floor. I am amazed. Her head looks like an egg. It is smooth and white and oval. She has no eyes, nose, mouth, hair, or ears.

"That's not so bad," I say, not wanting to hurt her feelings.

When I say this, there is movement within her head. It starts bulging and cracking. Eventually it transforms into the head of a beautiful human woman. I am very

strongly attracted to her in spite of her appearing some-
what cold.

"I want to make love to you," I tell her.

"No," she says.

"You will enjoy it," I say. She doesn't respond.

Somehow I persuade her to accompany me to another part of the building. We are standing, facing each other, in a shipping/receiving area next to large overhead doors. The doors are open. Outside is a large, empty parking lot.

"I want to make love to you," I say to her again.

"You can't," she says.

"Why not?" I ask.

"Because I have a penis," she says.

I am shocked to hear this and don't believe her. It angers me that she would tell me such a lie. I reach over with my right hand and rip off her skirt. She does have a penis! It looks like a young boy's penis. I am completely frustrated.

"Where did you get that?" I ask.

"I can change form," she says. "My last friend was female and had a tiny vagina, so I grew this tiny penis to fit her."

"Can you get rid of it and grow a vagina?" I ask.

"Yes," she says.

"Well, do it then," I tell her.

"No," she says.

"Why not?"

"I prefer being male," she says.

"Get rid of it! You will enjoy this."

Reluctantly, she complies. The penis disappears, and a vagina takes its place. I am amazed and pleased. I then gently kiss her mouth. It feels like kissing a machine. She is not responsive. After a while, though, she realizes that she likes being kissed and responds by kissing me, warmly. She becomes passionate. We quickly undress and engage in intercourse in a sitting position, our legs and arms wrapped around each other.

I very much enjoy holding her close to me and touching her, feeling her body next to mine, kissing her beautiful face. I especially enjoy squeezing her wonderful tush.

While we are making love, I notice an old man in the parking lot walking toward us. When he sees us, he stops, turns around, and begins walking away. As he does, two boys on bicycles approach. He stops them and tells them that they are not to play in this area and must leave. He is not harsh but firm, nevertheless, and they ride away. He feels that the intercourse the woman and I are engaged in is not child's play, that it is sacred, and the boys should not be present.

I want to know more about this woman with whom I'm entwined and ask, "Why did you come to Earth?"

"Communications," she says. I understand her to mean that her fellow aliens sent her here because they want Earth to be part of their communications network. They want a relationship with human beings.

The dream fades, and I awake feeling good but a bit overwhelmed.

❖   ❖   ❖

As I mentioned, immediately following the first dream that morning, it seemed to me that *Vita* was telling me that I had to die before I could unite with the women, and I consented to my demise. In the second dream, that consent was imaged, I think, as the dead fellow in the coffin-like hole in the basement floor—and that the so-strongly-desired union with the women was imaged as the intercourse with the transformed woman from outer space.

Vita had started "speaking" to me days before these two dreams, on the road to Kirksville, causing me to feel sad and disconnected from the life all around me. Having gotten my attention with the sadness, s/he imaged the problem in *The Women by the Pool*: Something in me, something imaged as the terminally ill men and boys, had to die before I could unite with something in me imaged as the women.

I later understood that what was doing me in, imaged as the dying males, a certain closed-offness, described years later as "numbed zone disorder":

A great problem for many men is that the chest is a numbed zone. Conditioned to shun feeling, avoid instinctual wisdom and *override* his inner truth, the average male is a stranger to himself and others, a slave to money, power and status. . . . When asked what he feels, a man will often explain what he thinks, or what the problem "out there" is. . . .

How can women expect to have good relationships with men when men do not have a relationship with their own feminine soul?[1]

After repeatedly asking *Vita* what s/he meant by the feminine figures in the dream, what finally popped up in my mind was something I had read years earlier:

Is this then what happens to woman? She wants perpetually to spill herself away. All her instinct as a woman—the eternal nourisher of children, of men, of society—demands that she give. Her time, her energy, her creativeness drain out into these channels if there is any chance, any leak. Traditionally we are taught, and instinctively we long, to give where it is needed—and immediately.[2]

1. James Hollis, *The Middle Passage: From Misery to Meaning in Midlife* (Toronto: Inner City Books, 1993), 53–54.

2. Anne Morrow Lindbergh, *Gift from the Sea*, intro. Reeve Lindbergh (New York: Pantheon Books, 1955, 2005), 39.

The women by the pool symbolized, as I understand it, "woman—the eternal nourisher of children, of men, of society . . . [who] give where it is needed—and immediately."

I was nurturing but not spontaneously so. That was the issue, I think, that *Vita* was addressing with the sadness on the road to Kirksville and with these two dreams.

I was lopsidedly analytical; I lived in my head too much. Brain removal was in order.

The dead man's cranium wasn't empty for long, however. The shape-shifting, masculine/feminine, womblike object soon appeared. It imaged my uniting with the "woman" within my soul, that is, with the spontaneity so long repressed, so alien to my numbed consciousness.

Again, the fulfilling of the desire for union, imaged as intercourse with the transformed, made-conscious alien woman, was made possible by the consent to my demise following *The Women by the Pool*—by my willingness to die, that is, to let go of my functioning as a numbed-out personality.

When s/he entered consciousness, the alien woman had a penis, which indicated, as I understand it, the extent to which my spontaneity had been stifled. The penis had to go, just as in *The Women by the Pool* the terminally ill male figures had to go, had to die. Its being small and childlike indicated, I think, that the problem, the squashed spontaneity, started when I was young boy.

Why did *Vita* care one way or another whether I became spontaneous, became whole? For the same reason s/he wanted the crucified man to rise up from the dead, and the ball of light brought up from the bottom of the sea, and the little boy released from his coffin: The life I am living, that each of us is living, is really hir life, and s/he wants to live it fully.

It has taken hir fourteen billion years to exist in human form, to create each of us. That is a lot of time and effort. Why should s/he *not* care?

Following the two dreams, I resolved to become spontaneous. I often laughed at myself, at the absurdity of the resolution. How was I to force myself to become spontaneous? It was not possible; it was contradictory. That didn't stop me from trying though.

I did the only thing I could come up with. I tried to stop thinking and just focus on whatever I was seeing, hearing, tasting, smelling, or touching. It didn't work at first, not at all. My mind kept jumping from one thought to another. But slowly, little by little, the incessant thinking lessened, and it became easier just to be.

Little things I had hardly noticed in the past I began to savor—Elyse's perfume, the aroma of coffee, multicolored sunsets, flowers, trees, birds, the feel of silk.

Elyse noticed the difference in me and loved it.

Recently, I came upon a poem that immediately brought to mind these two dreams and the feminine aspect of a man's soul. In the poem, the rower's experience of "She" is similar in effect to my experience of *Vita*:

The man who rowed across the ocean

He has decided to row across the Atlantic.
The boat is ready,
he has food and water for two months.
When he pushes off, a young woman appears,
with black hair, more beautiful
than any he has ever seen.
She says, "Take me along."
He knows it's the right thing to do,
the food will be enough for both of them.
He does not speak. She gets in.
The people on shore cry and cross themselves.

Soon he notices how She helps with the rowing.
Silence is her strength.
She talks to the fish and they jump into the boat.
She reads the sextant and tells him the direction.
She articulates what he thinks
and he thinks new thoughts.
Her strength is like a sail,
She converts all winds into forward energy.
When he rows he looks at her and does not tire.

When they finally sight Ireland
his eyes are healed by the Green.
No one has expected him this early.
It is calm and he completes the last few strokes
with his back to the land.

When he lands he is alone,
he had almost expected it.
But he knows that She will never leave him,
he knows it better than anything he has ever known.
He lets her name melt on his tongue daily.
It is nourishment for his entire being.[3]

---

3. Ulrich Schaffer, "The man who rowed across the ocean,"
   http://www.ulrich-schaffer.com/Poems.html.

Eleven
Life After Death

During the months following *The Women by the Pool* and *The Woman from Outer Space*, I enjoyed life so much that the thought of my eventual demise began weighing on me. I don't remember what triggered the thought.

I didn't want to cease existing, which is what was going to happen eventually, it seemed to me: no body, no mind, no existence. What permanent difference did it make whether I lived life authentically, whether I became whole? It was all going to end in the grave anyway. End of story.

Then one morning, a dream:

Life After Death
November 2, 1987

I am in a grocery store and see Joe, my best friend, a few aisles over! This can't be. Joe died several years ago.

I rush over to him. He looks healthy and content, not at all like the last time I saw him, glassy-eyed, thin, weak-voiced, breathing laboriously. He was thirty-three; so was I.

*When Joe sees me, he smiles and says hello. I ask
how he is, and he says he's fine. His voice is warm and
his eyes joyful. It's as if death were no big thing.*

*We walk down an aisle engaging in small talk. I
am momentarily distracted by a woman offering free
samples of something (I don't remember what). When
I turn back to him, he isn't there. I walk through the
store looking for him but don't see him anywhere. I am
disappointed. What is happening?*

*In one of the aisles, I see an old, white-haired,
distinguished-looking gentleman. He resembles a wise
psychiatrist whom I have either read about or met
somewhere. I walk up to him, introduce myself, and
ask whether he is a psychiatrist. He says he is.*

*I tell him about seeing Joe and talking to him and
say that I know this could not have actually happened
because he is dead and there's no life after death; how
could there be? I must be losing my mind, I say antic-
ipating his agreeing with me, but he doesn't. He is not
even surprised.*

*"If you want to understand seeing your deceased
friend again, you should read Bellarmine," he says. I
just look at him, speechless. I have no idea what he is
talking about.*

*Now I am in another part of the grocery store, talk-
ing to another friend, Bill. He has not died, as Joe had.
As a young man, he attended Kendrick-Glennon seminary in Shrewsbury for several years—the complex that*

once included the high school seminary I would have attended had I not changed my mind during the summer of 1959. Bill withdrew from the seminary shortly before he was to be ordained and then enrolled in law school, the same law school I attended, SLU. He is now a lawyer, but I think of him as a priest, a priest whose vocation is the pursuit of justice.

We are discussing the phenomena of sound and music.

Bill and I are now standing on the floor of a huge, empty arena, looking up at its high ceiling and the empty seats surrounding us. We are holding white circular disks resembling Frisbees. They are wrapped in clear plastic. We are also holding tuning forks. We climb the many steps to the top of the building and enter a large room. We sit on opposite ends of a couch, looking at the disks, and then remove the wrappers. Bill's disk is slightly damaged. I easily repair it by rubbing it with my hand.

We stand up and walk to opposite sides of the room, then face each other. We each hold the disk in one hand and the tuning fork in the other. I then strike my disk with the tuning fork. The disk begins glowing and emitting light and soft, soothing music. Then, Bill's tuning fork vibrates in sync with mine and his disk also emits light and music. I feel deeply peaceful.

As I awake, the dream seems realer than real, and I say to myself, "So there *really* is life after death!"

❖   ❖   ❖

I had been wrong about death being the end.

It wasn't the imagery of Joe's being alive again
that convinced me. It was understanding that *Vita* had
addressed the issue of life after death and told me there
was such, using imagery of Joe's being alive again to
convey hir message. Seeing him alive again after his
demise was, in effect, seeing myself alive again after
my own demise.

But there was something about the dream that baf-
fled me: the psychiatrist's advice to "read Bellarmine." I
tried many times to bring the name up in my memory
but couldn't and eventually gave up.

Several weeks after the dream, I was in a courtroom in Saint Louis observing a chemist testify. I was
lending a hand to a fellow assistant A.G. who had to
be elsewhere. Both of us represented the Missouri
Department of Natural Resources. He thought the
chemist might be helpful to him in a pollution case
he was handling involving the same toxin the chemist
was testifying about.

As I sat there and watched, the psychiatrist's advice
to read Bellarmine came to mind, and it occurred to me
that Pius XII Library was nearby, on the SLU campus.
What would come up, if anything, I wondered, were
I to look up "Bellarmine" in the card catalog? Maybe
Bellarmine, whoever he was, had written something
about life after death.

When the chemist finished testifying, I visited
the library. As I entered, memories of long-forgotten
events and conversations surfaced, one in particular.
I remembered Joe's saying in response to something
I had said, "God damn it, Steinmann, you're always
looking for The Answer! There is no Answer. Haven't
you figured that out yet? Just live life and stop trying
to comprehend everything." How strange it felt being
there again, recalling that conversation, one that had
occurred over a quarter century earlier, still looking
for The Answer. Was Joe looking down at me now,
smiling?

Looking through the cards, one jumped out. On it
was the name "Bellarmine" and the name of a book
published in 1622, *The Art of Dying Well.* There on the
card was a connection between Bellarmine and death,
the theme of the dream. Was this really happening?

Long ago a nun or priest must have mentioned
Bellarmine and what he had written about death, I
thought, and although I had forgotten it, *Vita* had
not—just as I had forgotten μετανοια but s/he had not.
I found a copy of *The Art of Dying Well* in the stacks
and, after obtaining an alumnus library card, checked
it out.

Chapter XVII, the concluding chapter, contains
Bellarmine's comparison of certain biblical characters
who led virtuous lives and others who didn't. The former entered into eternal bliss when they died and the

latter into eternal damnation. The former were blissful because they had perfected the state into which they had been called by God.[1]

"Read Bellarmine" was *Vita's* way of telling me that it matters to hir whether I perfect the state into which I had been called, that is, whether I correctly translate the difficult manuscript, the script I came into the world with.

That it matters to hir was all I really needed to know.

I wonder, did the first Jesus followers, living in a culture in which people believed that God and "his" angels appeared to them in dreams and visions, have dreams similar to this one, dreams so vivid they were convinced that their friend, Jesus, was alive again?

---

1. Robert Bellarmine, *The Art of Dying Well*, ed. E. M. Rogers (London: Scolar Press, 1976), 327–28.

Twelve
The Rifle
Together Again

December 1988–March 1989

In December 1988, an earthquake struck Spitak, Armenia, killing thousands. Watching the news reports, I was horrorstruck.

At the time I was taking a church-sponsored Bible-study course. Where was almighty Yahweh when the earthquake struck? Why did he not prevent it?

In March 1989 another earthquake was in the news, and it brought to a head the issue I was struggling with: God's power and hir culpability or the lack thereof. On the one hand, I knew *Vita*, whom I had been experiencing as God for four years, was loving and healing, but on the other, the earthquakes *had* occurred. How loving and healing was that?

During the day preceding the next dream, I repeatedly asked *Vita* whether s/he possessed the power to have prevented the quakes, and as best I could tell by paying attention to my feelings, the answer was no. My feelings weren't dispositive, of course; maybe

I was deluding myself. Nevertheless, I felt *Vita* had responded, and I was comforted.

In addition to the issue of God's culpability, something else was running through my mind at the time: a fantasy of hunting elk in a wilderness area high up in the Rockies. I daydreamed about what gear to take with me, and in particular, which rifle; there were so many manufacturers, models, and calibers.

Looking back, I see that underlying the elk-hunting fantasy was my desire for an experience similar to what I understood Native Americans long ago had after a successful hunt—a deep communion with the life-giving Great Spirit, a deep gratitude for the food that sustained them. I think the Bible-study course was a factor in my having the fantasy. The fantasy was an escape from the Bible; I had a hard time relating to stories I didn't believe were true.

I should not have taken the course. It was designed for people who were convinced that the Bible was the word of God and who wanted to spread the word, who wanted to teach the Bible to others. That wasn't me; I just wanted it to be. I wanted to believe but still needed to be persuaded; I had hoped the course would result in belief. It didn't.

The Rifle
March 8, 1989, 3 a.m.
I am in the Missouri State Capitol, standing in front of huge courtroom doors, waiting for the judge

to arrive. Several other men are present. One of them is the Director of Administration, the others, his subordinates. I am disgusted and angry with the director and have filed a lawsuit against him; he had ordered that my beautiful black hunting bow be taken from me. I want it back, to use it someday to hunt elk in the Rockies. He took it because I have a disability of some sort and am presently unable to hunt. I think his taking the bow was unfair.

When the judge arrives, everyone enters the courtroom. The director takes the witness stand, and I tear into him, accusing him of being an insensitive, inept, unjust fool. This goes on for quite a while. The judge listens to me and the director's responses and agrees with me; the bow was taken from me unfairly. He orders the director to retrieve it and return it. He says that whether I was able to hunt was not relevant; the bow was mine regardless.

I am pleased. The director and his subordinates are embarrassed.

The subordinates and I are now in a large department store operated by the Office of Administration, standing next to cash registers in the checkout area. His men don't know where the bow is or how to retrieve it. I remember that there is a number on it, and I give it to them, and they trace the bow through a computerized cash register. They will soon return it to me.

I ask the cashier about a rifle I ordered sometime in the past. I don't remember anything about it except that it had to be inexpensive because I'm not wealthy. The cashier walks over to some boxes and returns with one with my name on it. She opens the box and pulls out a rifle.

I can hardly believe my eyes, the rifle is a work of art! The receiver is beautifully engraved and the stock and forearm magnificently carved. It must be worth a fortune. As I examine it, I can't recall ever reading or hearing about a rifle like this one, an over/under double, the top barrel chambered in .270 caliber and the bottom in .30-06. It must be unique. I would love to have it with me in the Rockies.

The cashier tells me that her checking out the rifle would require her to work overtime and that she has to leave. I say that's fine; I'll return tomorrow. Then somehow I am at another register where time is not a factor, and the rifle is rung up. The price is minimal. I can actually afford it. The rifle must be a gift from someone who has made up the difference between the small amount I am paying and the rifle's actual value. The clerk hands the rifle to me.

The dream fades, and I awake feeling good, especially about owning the magnificent gun.

As I record the dream in my journal, the Book of Job comes to mind. Job had dialogued with God about his unfair treatment, and I too had been dialoguing with *Vita* the day before the dream about the unfair treatment of the residents of Spitak. What had they done wrong to deserve the devastating quake? I remembered that at the end of the Book, Job was gifted by God with a new family and possessions, and at the end of the dream I was gifted by *Vita* with the magnificent rifle.

Had *Vita* appreciated my dialoguing with hir the day before, confronting hir with God's apparent indifference and, as a reward, had given me the rifle?

I fall asleep. Three hours later, a second dream.

Together Again
March 8, 1989, 6 a.m.

I am at a party and see across the room a beautiful, sophisticated woman, a childhood friend whom I haven't seen in many years. I am immediately and strongly attracted to her. She is now a clinical psychologist. In her warm, radiant eyes I see that she is very closely connected to the divine.

As I approach her, an old man with whom she had been talking is walking away from her. She says to someone nearby that the man is depressed and that she is concerned about him.

She smiles when I am close to her. I don't know whether she recognizes me or is just being friendly. I say, "I haven't seen you in so many years, I bet you don't remember me. I'm Ed Steinmann."

"How are you?" she asks. From the warmth in her eyes and voice, it's apparent she does remember me and is genuinely happy to see me. I feel as if I have been reunited with a long-lost part of myself.

"Just fine, thanks," I say. "One thing I'm into these days is dreams. I have had some wonderful dreams."

"Dreams are the world," she says, and her eyes become even more radiant. I think about what she has just said but don't understand it. I see, however, that she knows exactly what she is talking about. (She says something else, but I can't remember it.)

The woman and I are now in a hallway, leaving the party together. We belong together and know it. Her love for me is as deep as mine for her. We are happy.

The dream fades, and I wake up feeling wonderful, thinking that I had been gifted a second time that morning—the first gift being the rifle, the second the reunion with the close-to-the-divine woman, my childhood friend—a gift for having understood, at least a little, the first dream that morning.

There are no courtrooms in the Missouri Capitol, only the House and Senate chambers, the legislators' offices, the governor's office, several hearing rooms, a museum, a cafeteria, and so on.

I think *Vita* included a courtroom in *The Rifle* to symbolize almightiness, that is, all the power that exists—legislative, executive, judicial, being under one roof. The courtroom by itself did not express almightiness, just the opposite. It expressed limited power, the limited power of a judge to interpret the law—power that doesn't extend to enacting law or enforcing it.

The Director of Administration was a personification, it seems to me, of the law according to which the Universe is apparently administered—survival of the fittest. It was according to that administrative rule that my hunting bow was taken from me. I was unfit to hunt, and so the director took the bow.

The judge reversed the director's decision and ordered the bow returned but didn't say why. Apparently there is a higher law at work in the Universe, one to which the survival-of-the-fittest rule is subordinate.

What I think *Vita* was telling me was that, if s/he had the power to reverse the Spitak earthquake, s/he would because it was unfair to the residents of Spitak—just as the taking of my bow was unfair, and s/he, imaged as the judge, reversed that taking.

Vita is not culpable with respect to natural catastrophes and other heartbreakers; that is my understanding, my interpretation, of the dream.

What is the higher law pursuant to which the judge reversed the director's survival-of-the-fittest administrative rule? Again, it wasn't spelled out in the dream. But it now appears to me, because of the books I read later, that the basic law at work in the Universe, to which the survival-of-the-fittest administrative rule is subordinate, is that of attraction-cooperation, termed "love" by some, the result of which is an evolving, increasingly complex, increasingly conscious world, a world that produces novelty, that produced us.[1]

In *Together Again* the woman said, "Dreams are the world," but I didn't understand. Sometime later, the following popped up in my mind:

> O chestnut-tree, great-rooted blossomer,
> Are you the leaf, the blossom or the bole?
> O body swayed to music, O brightening glance,
> How can we know the dancer from the dance?[2]

Is *Vita* the dancer and we the dance; s/he the dreamer and we the dream? Was every person killed or injured by the Spitak quake actually *Vita* in human form?

That thought does not take away the pain, but it does give me pause. I'm not keen as I once was to

---

1. Pierre Teilhard de Chardin, SJ, "The Spirit of the Earth," in *Human Energy*, trans. J. M. Cohen (New York: Harcourt Brace Jovanovich, 1962, 1969), 34; see also John Haught, *God After Darwin: A Theology of Evolution* (Boulder, Colorado: Westview Press, 2000); and, Carter Phipps, *Evolutionaries: Unlocking the Spiritual and Cultural Potential of Science's Greatest Idea* (New York: Harper Perennial, 2012).
2. William Butler Yeats, "Among School Children," in *The Tower* (1928; Project Gutenberg Australia, 2006), http://gutenberg.net.au/ebooks06/0608541.txt.

prosecute God for crimes against humanity. It may be that this world with all of its unmerited suffering is the only one in which we human beings, could have come into being. Would I annihilate the Universe if I could because unmerited suffering exists?

No.

Thirteen
The Real Presence

A few days after *The Rifle* and *Together Again*, I shared both dreams with a friend, explaining their meaning as best I could. The following morning:

The Real Presence
March 17, 1989

I am a priest saying mass in the church of my youth, Saint Gabriel the Archangel in Saint Louis. I feel at home, saying mass here. I am happy. When I am finished at the altar, I walk over to the pulpit and bless the parishioners with the sign of the cross and say, "Go in peace; the mass is ended."

I join the parishioners as they walk through the nave and vestibule and out the front door, chatting with several of them and enjoying their company. When most of them have left, I walk down the front steps to the sidewalk. A priest who was one of my religion teachers in high school joins me. He looks much the same as he did then.

He asks how I am, and I say I feel very good, I feel close to God, even though I'm no longer a Catholic. He

is troubled and asks me why I left the church. I say it is
because I don't believe many of the things the church
teaches. I don't elaborate but am thinking of Fall/
Redemption theology in particular. He doesn't under-
stand my attitude, and I don't try to explain; he has no
interest in dreams and visions. He shakes his head in
disappointment, wishing I were still Catholic. He walks
away.

I am now walking through the parish grammar
school next to the church, which I attended for nine
years, from kindergarten through eighth grade. I hav-
en't been in the school in decades. Walking down a
hall, I look into a classroom and see myself as a child
sitting at a desk. Seeing my young self, I realize that I
have fulfilled the promise of my youth. I have fulfilled
my destiny. I am the priest I was intended to be. I feel
ineffably, paradisiacally wonderful.

As the dream fades away, I remember feeling this
bliss once before, at the conclusion of the *Abba* dream,
after having assumed my father's ministry.

In sharing *The Rifle* and *Together Again*, I was
apparently, in *Vita's* eyes, functioning as a priest, not
the Catholic priest I had wanted to be thirty years earlier but, a priest in the sense of a bridge between hir
and my friend. Was that what s/he wanted from me
all along, my destiny in other words, my being such
a bridge? Is that what s/he wants from each of us to

some extent, our bridging the gap between hir and consciousness and our sharing such experiences?

But why a priest *saying mass?*

The heart of the mass is the Eucharist, the piece of bread consumed during communion. Ingesting it, I was taught, is ingesting Jesus, taking God into our body and soul, the bread having been "transubstantiated" via a miracle into Jesus' body. The teaching is rooted, in part, in the words attributed to Jesus during the Last Supper before his execution:

> Then he [Jesus] took a loaf of bread, and when he had given thanks, he broke it and gave it to them, saying, "This is my body, which is given for you. Do this in remembrance of me." (Luke 22:19, 20)

> So Jesus said to them, "Very truly, I tell you, unless you eat the flesh of the Son of Man and drink his blood, you have no life in you. Those who eat my flesh and drink my blood have eternal life, and I will raise them up on the last day; for my flesh is true food and my blood is true drink. Those who eat my flesh and drink abide in me, and I in them. Just as the living Father sent me, and I live because of the Father, so whoever eats me will live because of me. This is the bread that came down from heaven, not like that which our ancestors ate, and they

died. But the one who eats this bread will live
forever. (John 6:53–58)

I don't believe Jesus uttered these words. I believe
they were put in his mouth by his followers and rep-
resent their effort to make sense of his significance for
them. The passages were shaped by earlier Jewish stories, practices, and beliefs, such as the Passover meal
and the Bread of the Presence, the belief that God was
present in a special bread kept in a tabernacle.[1]

Although I don't believe the communion host
(bread) is Jesus' body, I do believe ingesting God, so
to speak, does occur. It was imaged in *The Call* in the
dream ego's descent to the bottom of the sea, swallow-
ing the ball of light and bringing it up to the surface.

Is that why *Vita* imaged me as a priest saying
mass? Is that what communion is *really* all about, in
hir opinion, bringing hir up to the surface, enabling hir
to become conscious, to incarnate? Was I doing that,
bringing hir up to the surface, in relating and explaining for my friend, and for myself also, the *The Rifle* and
Together Again?

Which brings me to something Pope Francis said:

. . . St. Vincent of Lerins makes a comparison
between the biological development of man and
the transmission from one era to another of the

---

1   Brant Pitre, *Jesus and the Jewish Roots of the Eucharist* (New York:
    Doubleday Religion, 2011).

deposit of faith, which grows and is strengthened in time. Here, human self-understanding changes with time and so also human consciousness deepens.[2]

My human consciousness and self-understanding have certainly deepened over the years, as has my understanding of the "deposit of faith"—the scriptures, traditions, and teachings of the church. I see the deposit as a rich, two-thousand-year outpouring of, projection of, inner realities onto external people and events via various stories, dogmas, sacraments, rituals, and so on. The deposit should not be discarded but rather reinterpreted in light of the growth in human self-understanding.

The teaching regarding transubstantiation, for example, should be seen as a projection of the change, the transubstantiation, if you will, that takes place in us when we bring *Vita* up from the depths and embody hir.

---

2 Antonio Spadaro, *A Big Heart Open to God: A Conversation with Pope Francis*, foreword by Matt Malone, SJ (published by the editors of *America*, 2013), Kindle edition, loc. 495 (chap. "Human Self-Understanding").

Fourteen
The Faith that Saves

I was in turmoil, trying to compose a letter terminating our membership in the church, the church that Elyse and I had loved so much when we joined seven years earlier. We realized finally, painfully, that we didn't belong. We didn't believe the Bible to be the word of God, although we had tried hard to believe. We dropped out of the Bible-study course just before it ended. It was a two-year program.

I, an ex-Catholic, was to become an ex-Protestant also. That realization didn't sit well with me at all. Was I about to become utterly irreligious?

The next morning, a dream:

The Faith That Saves
October 19, 1990

I am in a schoolroom looking at a nun in the hallway. She is dressed in her habit and standing on a chair in front of a row of huge lockers. She leans forward, and I notice that she is pregnant. She is fastening a cord to a hook high above her. She is preparing to hang herself!

The nun and I are now walking along a path through a field adjoining a forest. She tells me about an order of nuns in a foreign country that cares for babies born to nuns; she is going to give her baby to them. I find it odd and confusing that there are so many nuns having babies that a whole order exists to take care of them. The nuns tell the children that God is their father.

I mention an alternative: she could leave the convent and marry the baby's father. When I say this, an image of him appears in my mind. He is an impressive-looking, successful, aggressive businessman, highly regarded in the business community, but he has no depth, no insight, no interior spiritual life. All he cares about is money. The nun tells me there is no way she could marry him; she couldn't stand living with him. I empathize with her.

I am now alone, walking through the forest, and see a snake on the ground near a tree. It must be someone's pet, I think, because the area surrounding the tree, two or three feet in diameter, resembles a cage or nest someone has prepared for it. There are no bars or wires or anything else confining the snake to the prepared area, yet it is supposed to stay there. How bizarre, I think, that anyone would think that the snake would stay in this small spot. Whoever made this "cage," expecting the snake to stay put, is really stupid.

I want to play with the snake. I throw a rock or twig near it to get its attention. It wiggles around. It also wants to play. I throw some more things near it, and it wiggles some more.

Now I'm walking through another part of the forest. The snake appears on the path in front of me. It wants to play. I throw something close to it, and it moves. This time, however, it moves through the air. The snake is flying! It doesn't have wings but nevertheless flies through the air. It is dancing! Watching the snake, I am amazed and amused. I really like this little snake.

I am now close to a large house alongside the forest. I walk through a back door and enter the kitchen. It is large and resembles the kitchen of the house I grew up in. A fundamentalist preacher is in the kitchen, standing to my right, near the sink. I have seen him on television. I know somehow that he thinks of the snake as his; he thinks he owns it.

I notice the kitchen table. It is set with a tablecloth, dishes, silverware, and so on. It is clean and neat.

I am holding in my hand a small branch of a tree containing several smaller branches. They are full of tiny pieces of meat and gristle. I am looking forward to eating it.

The preacher says that we are going to have a nice, big dinner in the kitchen and that it will be much better than the meaty stick. He tells me to get rid of it. I don't want to. I'd rather be in the forest with the snake and

*the meaty stick than in the kitchen with the preacher
and his fine dinner.*

*I am now in a clearing in the forest with a group
of women having a picnic. There is a blackboard near
the picnic table. I tell the women about my experience
with the friendly snake and ask if someone would like
to draw a picture on the blackboard of what the snake
means.*

*One woman steps up to the blackboard. I know
her. She is a member of a fundamentalist church. She
draws a picture on the blackboard. (I can't remember
the picture.)*

"That wasn't your first choice, was it?" I say to her.

"No, it wasn't," she responds.

"Well, erase it then and draw your first choice," I say.

*She erases it and draws a picture of a doll, a baby
girl. "Why didn't you want to draw this picture?" I ask.*

*"I didn't want the snake to be so humanlike," she
says, fear in her voice.*

*"You mean you didn't want the snake to be in
control?"*

"That's right," she says.

*She then pauses. She is thinking about something.
Her eyes soon brighten; she is understanding something
for the first time. The drawing on the blackboard turns
into an actual doll and is now in the woman's arms.
She is no longer fearful but happy and smiling broadly.*

The dream ends, and I awake, feeling good.

A pregnant nun about to hang herself?

She was, I think, an image of my soul impregnated and compromised by materialism, imaged as the businessman. Leaving the church, was that what was to become of me—spiritually compromised, materialistic, unhappy, suicidal?

The fundamentalist woman and the preacher represented the part of me that, despite my disbelief, still wanted to cling to the Bible as God's word, the part of me that would confine the snake (Nature, Reality, God) to a small "cage," that of Biblical literalism, fearing I would be overwhelmed were I to forever give up any hope of believing the Bible to be the word of God.

What was it that the fundamentalist woman eventually understood, imaged by her brightening eyes and the drawing's becoming an actual doll she joyfully held? It was, I think, that the snake was friendly, was not to be feared.

When thinking about what that meant, these words popped up in my mind: *The faith that saves is the ego's trust of the unconscious*—meaning that I would still have faith, trust, in *Vita*, and that that trust was sufficient. I must have been thinking secularly that day, given the terminology. My anxiety lessened.

Karl Rahner, the highly influential twentieth century Catholic theologian, said in an interview that ". . . the devout Christian of the future will either be a 'mystic,' one who has 'experienced' something, or he will cease to be anything at all."[1] Had I become such, "a devout Christian of the future," by the time of this dream despite my disbelief in both Catholicism and Protestantism, someone who had *experienced something* deeply within myself rather than externally through indoctrination?[2]

1. Karl Rahner, "Christian Living Formerly and Today," in *Theological Investigations Volume VII: Further Theology of the Spiritual Life 1*, trans. David Bourke (London: Darton, Longman & Todd, 1971), 15.

2. Karl Rahner, "Contemporary Youth and the Experience of God," an interview with Hubert Biallowons and Ferdinand Herget, in *Faith in a Wintry Season: Conversations and Interviews with Karl Rahner in the Last Years of His Life*, eds. Paul Imhof and Hubert Biallowons, trans. Harvey D. Egan, SJ (New York: Crossroad Pub. Co., 1991). 107; Karl Rahner, *Foundations of Christian Faith: An Introduction to the Idea of Christianity* (New York: Crossroad Publishing Co., 2002), 229.

Fifteen

Some Thoughts on the Imagery in *Face To Face*

I will return now to the various images in the vision. I hope my comments make more sense now than they would have earlier. To refresh your memory, the images were, in their order of appearance:

- a tiny white circle
- numerous tiny white circles spinning, spiraling, swirling, dancing
- a child playing with Roman candles on the Fourth of July
- white lines in the form of an eye
- an "I"
- a cross
- a man hanging on the cross
- a rectangular box resembling a coffin
- the coffin with a man rising up out of it, smiling, joyful
- the risen man, glorious, ball of white light in his chest, walking, facing me
- oval-shaped white lines, resembling a vulva
- the oval-shaped lines penetrated by a white shaft

- the white shaft containing several white dots
- a large white circle containing one small white circle
- a large white circle containing seven small white circles
- a large white circle resembling a planet, with seven newborns, seeing the world for the first time
- a tiny red ball
- a white flash
- tiny white dots slowly appearing, seeming to image the creation of the universe, to image evolution

Followed by: "What are you trying to tell me?"
"I — am — you."

My current understanding of the imagery:

The tiny white circle: oneness with *Vita*, the dream-vision creator.

The little circle was an image of the state of consciousness, or mode of self, existing during the vision, referred to by some as unitive or nondual consciousness; oneness with "the Power of the World." In Black Elk's words: "You have noticed that everything an Indian does is in a circle, and that is because the Power of the World always works in circles, and everything tries to be round."[1]

---

1. John Neihardt, *Black Elk Speaks* (New York: Pocket Books, 1959), 164.

The dancing circles: *Vita*'s ecstatic response to my returning to hir.

In the prodigal son parable (Luke 15:11–32), the son takes his inheritance early and blows it on loose living. Then, lost and alone in an alien land, he yearns to return home and does so, and instead of being turned away his return is celebrated.

In putting myself in a deep state of relaxation and opening up to being penetrated by the dream creator, I was like the prodigal son returning home to his parent—that parable actually being about our conscious return to our parent, *Vita*.

As I understand it, when we are in our mother's womb, we are one with Nature, *Vita*, but not consciously so. In the course of growing up we become increasingly independent, increasingly disconnected from hir. In the vision, I was once again one with hir, once again connected, but this time, unlike in the womb, consciously so.

Which brings me to Fall/Redemption theology. Could the Fall actually be rooted in our expulsion when we are born from subconscious, paradisiacal oneness in the womb, and our Redemption rooted in the experience of conscious oneness later in life—when we let go, when we die on a cross, so to speak?

If the church cannot discard Fall/Redemption theology, or doesn't wish to, can that theology be reinterpreted to accord with a contemporary understanding of reality—of embryonic oneness, its loss, and its eventual, conscious recovery and an eventual conscious oneness?

The child playing with Roman candles on the Fourth of July: independence; freedom from the gloom of disconnectedness.

The eye: oneness.

As Meister Eckhart put it:

"The eye with which I see God is the same as the eye with which God sees me: my eye and God's eye are one eye, one seeing, one knowing and one love."[2]

The capital letter "I": *Vita*'s explicitly identifying hirself, announcing hir presence.

"Be still, and know that I am God!" (Psalm 46:10)

The cross: our destiny.

Our destiny is to develop a strong, apparently independent ego and then to "sacrifice" it, to let go of its illusory independence, in order to enable *Vita*, Life, to enter into consciousness. The cross, displayed in every Christian church in the world, symbolizes *our* destiny:

> For those who want to save their life will lose it, and those who lose their life for my sake will find it. (Matthew 16:35)

---

2. Meister Eckhart, *The Complete Mystical Works of Meister Eckhart*, ed. and trans. Maurice O'Connell Walshe, foreword by Bernard McGinn (New York: Crossroad Pub. Co., 2009), 298.

The man dying on the cross: what letting go of the ego's exclusivity feels like.

The rectangle/coffin: the transitional place in my soul where transformation, from death to life, from disconnectedness to connectedness, was taking place.

The man arising from the coffin, ecstatic, smiling: consciousness connecting with *Vita*.

In Saint Paul's words:

When this perishable body puts on imperisha-bility, and this mortal body puts on immortality, then the saying that is written will be fulfilled:
"Death has been swallowed up in victory."
Where, O death, is your victory?
Where, O death, is your sting?
(1 Corinthians 15:54, 55)

The risen Christ figure, looking at me face to face, dust on his shoes, strong, having the same loving, joyful, wise eyes of the defendant in *But Now My Eye Sees You*, looking a bit like me if I were God in human form, a ball of light in his chest: oneness.

He was an image of the state of consciousness, or mode of self, existing during the vision: human/divine oneness, so to speak.

Did Saint Paul see similar imagery? Some of the things he said make me think so:

I have been crucified with Christ; and it is no longer I who live, but it is Christ who lives in me. (Galatians 2:19–20)

And all of us, with unveiled faces, seeing the glory of the Lord as though reflected in a mirror, are being transformed into the same image from one degree of glory to another; for this comes from the Lord, the Spirit. (2 Corinthians 3:18)

We know that our old self was crucified with him. (Romans 6:6)

. . . he appeared to me. (1 Corinthians 15:8)

Have I not seen Jesus our Lord? (1 Corinthians 9:1)

In their case the god of this world has blinded the minds of the unbelievers, to keep them from seeing the light of the gospel of the glory of Christ, who is the likeness of God. For what we preach is not ourselves, but Jesus Christ as Lord, with ourselves as your servants for Jesus' sake. For it is the God who said, "Let light shine out of darkness," who has shone in our hearts to give the light of the knowledge of the glory of God in the face of Christ. (2 Corinthians 4:4–6)

But you are not in the flesh; you are in the Spirit, since the Spirit of God dwells in you.

Anyone who does not have the Spirit of Christ does not belong to him. But if Christ is in you, though the body is dead because of sin, the Spirit is life because of righteousness. If the Spirit of him who raised Jesus from the dead dwells in you, he who raised Christ from the dead will give life to your mortal bodies also through his Spirit that lives in you. (Romans 8:9—11)

So is it with the resurrection of the dead. What is sown is perishable; what is raised is imperishable. (1 Corinthians 15:42)

For if we have been united with him in a death like his, we will certainly be united with him in a resurrection like his. (Romans 6:5)

For now we see in a mirror, dimly, but then we will see face to face. Now I know only in part; then I will know fully, even as I have been fully known. And now faith, hope, and love abide, these three; and the greatest of these is love. (1 Corinthians 13:12, 13)

Do not lie to one another, seeing that you have stripped off the old self with its practices and have clothed yourselves with the new self, which is being renewed in knowledge according to the image of its creator. In that renewal there is no longer Greek and Jew, circumcised and uncircumcised, barbarian, Scythian, slave and free; but Christ is all, and in all. (Colossians 3:9–11)

For to me, living is Christ and dying is gain. (Philippians 1:21)

From now on, therefore, we regard no one from a human point of view; even though we once knew Christ from a human point of view, we know him no longer in that way. So if anyone is in Christ, there is a new creation: everything old has passed away; see, everything has become new. All this is from God, who reconciled us to himself through Christ. (2 Corinthians 5:16–18)

What do you think? Was Jesus the projection-carrier of Paul's own inner death and resurrection, his own experience of oneness, the "new creation" of which he spoke in 2 Corinthians 5:16—18 (and Galatians 6:15)? Was this new creation a new mode of self, a new consciousness resulting from the merger of *Vita* and Paul?

Was the risen Christ figure in my vision, looking a bit like me if I were divine, an image of such new creation?

Is *Vita*, experienced by me in the twentieth and twenty-first centuries as the dream-vision creator, an equivalent term for Paul's "life-giving Spirit" (in Romans

8: 9—11)? Are *Vita* and the Holy Spirit the same entity, just conceptualized differently?

The vulva-shaped white lines: receptivity, mine and *Vita's*.

The vulva (vagina) penetrated by the phallus: oneness.

The phallus containing the white dots: potency, mine and *Vita's*; the ability to bring forth new life, new consciousness, a new mode of self.

The three images—the vulva, the vulva (vagina) penetrated by the phallus, and the phallus—looks to me like a union-of-opposites trinity. Is God a union-of-loving-opposites trinity?

The imagery also looks to me to be a representation of *Vita* and I united in intercourse, resulting in a third mode of being: a merger resulting in oneness.

Are we made in God's image?

The circle containing one small circle: *Vita's* being pregnant with a new, self-reflective consciousness, mine/hirs, resulting from our intercourse.

The circle containing seven small circles: *Vita's* being fully pregnant, my being as conscious as it was possible for me to be.

"Earth" with seven newborns: born-againness, the transformation of consciousness from disconnectedness to connectedness.

Did Jesus and his followers see imagery such as this?

> The Spirit joins with our spirit to bear common witness that we are children of God. (Romans 8:16)

> Very truly, I tell you, no one can see the kingdom of God without being born from above. (John 3:3)

> The Kingdom of God is not coming with things that can be observed; nor will they say, "Look, here it is!" or "There it is!" For, in fact, the kingdom of God is among [within] you. (Luke 17:20, 21)

The tiny red ball in the center of blackness: the no-time/no-space/no-thing Mystery, Being hirself, God, existing before flashing into being, at least in part, as the Universe.

The white flash: creation; the Mystery, God, incarnating, transforming hirself, at least in part, into the Universe.

The blackness following the white flash: an imageless awareness-feeling of being enveloped in, contained in, an embracing Presence.

The white specks appearing one after another: the Universe's unfolding, evolving.

"I — am — you": "I, the tiny red ball, the Mystery, God, am the Universe and everything and everyone in it, including you."

I was dumbfounded at first when I heard "I — am — you." It seemed that *Vita,* the mind-entity creating the vision, whom I experienced as God, was telling me that I was God, which made no sense at all. It did inflate me, however, briefly. Then it angered me. If there was one thing I knew for certain, it was that I was not God. I could not create a toenail much less the Universe, so how could *Vita* have told me such an outrageous lie?

Later, I understood *Vita* to have said that s/he was the Universe and everything, everyone, in it. That insight has changed the way I look at the world. Everything I see I recognize as the tiny red ball fourteen billion years after the Big Bang.

That insight has also enabled me to understand this biblical passage, which I did not grasp previously:

> When the Son of Man comes in his glory, and all the angels with him, then he will sit on the throne of his glory. All the nations will be gathered before him, and he will separate people one from another as a shepherd separates the sheep from the goats, and he will put the sheep at his right hand and the goats at the left. Then the king will say to those at his right hand, "Come, you that are blessed by

my Father, inherit the kingdom prepared for
you from the foundation of the world; for I was
hungry and you gave me food, I was thirsty
and you gave me something to drink, I was a
stranger and you welcomed me, I was naked
and you gave me clothing, I was sick and you
took care of me, I was in prison and you visited
me." Then the righteous will answer him, "Lord,
when was it that we saw you hungry and gave
you food, or thirsty and gave you something
to drink? And when was it that we saw you a
stranger and welcomed you, or naked and gave
you clothing? And when was it that we saw
you sick or in prison and visited you?" And the
king will answer them, "Truly I tell you, just as
you did it to one of the least of these who are
members of my family, you did it to me." Then
he will say to those at his left hand, "You that
are accursed, depart from me into the eternal
fire prepared for the devil and his angels; for
I was hungry and you gave me no food, I was
thirsty and you gave me nothing to drink, I was
a stranger and you did not welcome me, naked
and you did not give me clothing, sick and in
prison and you did not visit me." Then they also
will answer, 'Lord, when was it that we saw
you hungry or thirsty or a stranger or naked or
sick or in prison, and did not take care of you?"
Then he will answer them, "Truly I tell you, just

as you did not do it to one of the least of these, you did not do it to me." And these will go away into eternal punishment, but the righteous into eternal life. (Matthew 25:31–46)

It is not important to me whether Jesus spoke these words or similar words or they were put in his mouth by others, or that the terms used, such as Son of Man, are not terms I would use. It is the perspective underlying the passage that I find important: What is done for the lowliest is done for the tiny red ball, God, because s/he is the lowliest as well as the highest, but as the lowliest, the neediest, s/he suffers more and is more appreciative when someone lends hir a helping hand.

Sixteen
The Woman in Grandfather's House

Driving down a country road, looking at the horses, goats, trees, clouds, and all, realizing everything I was seeing was, in one form or another, the tiny red ball fourteen billion years after having flashed into being as the Universe, realizing that my body was actually the red ball's body, my brain hir brain, everything mine hirs—except for the choices I make—I felt so very alive and joyful.

I understood that the joy I was feeling was actually hirs, that s/he deeply loved having arrived at this point after so long, evolving slowly all the while, understood how deeply s/he was appreciating the moment, the oneness existing in hir-me.

The next morning, a dream:

The Woman in Grandfather's House
May 29, 2012

I am riding an electric motor bike or scooter on a street in St. Louis. I stop in front of the big house my grandfather built before I was born, my childhood home. The front yard is terraced, and I walk up the

*concrete steps to the porch and up the wooden porch
steps to the front door and knock. A woman about thirty
years old opens the door. A young child is with her in the
living room a few feet away. I introduce myself and say
that this house was built by my grandfather and that I
grew up here and am just reminiscing and would like
to see the inside of the house once again, if it would not
be too much trouble. She invites me in.*

*The interior of the house has been changed; several
walls have been removed. The first floor is now open,
not divided as it was originally. The heavy wooden
sliding doors separating the dining room and the hall
are gone along with the walls that contained them. The
ceiling in the area that had been the dining room is
covered with reddish metal tile, unlike originally.*

*The woman takes me through the house for half
an hour or so, through the first and second floors and
basement. I am appreciative.*

*We are standing in the center of the house on the
first floor in what used to be the hall. There is a wall
near us, containing two doors, one leading upstairs to
the bedrooms and the other to the basement. It is time
for me to leave.*

*I feel like giving the woman an appreciative hug but
hesitate. She might think that I am coming on to her,
which wouldn't be the case; I would just like to express
my gratitude for her allowing me to tour the house.
Eventually I overcome my misgivings and give her a
little hug.*

I am surprised by her reaction when I begin to draw back. She pulls me closer! She does not want me to leave her. Her feelings are intense, to say the least. I feel them. Realizing she wants more from me, I kiss her softly on the forehead and again begin to draw back. She will have none of it. She pulls me even closer.

The dream fades, and I awake feeling the woman's intense desire that I remain with her.

Every morning since this dream I do what I think the woman in my grandfather's house—in my great Father's house—wants me to do; I hold her close. After paying attention to whatever dream is running through my mind, I lie in bed and recall the woman's passion and reflect upon the fact that, except for the choices I make, everything I usually think of as mine is actually *Vita's*—my feet, legs, arms, hands, eyes, brain, consciousness, everything—and I am grateful to exist in this form, to be human, to be in this relationship.

Sometimes, later in the day I feel so good, so connected, warm and at home with *Vita* that I wonder whether this is what heaven feels like.

I understand what Fr. Pedro Arrupe, SJ, meant when he wrote the following, although we arrived at this place walking different paths:

Fall in Love
Nothing is more practical than
finding God, than

falling in Love
in a quite absolute, final way.

What you are in love with
what seizes your imagination, will affect
everything.

It will decide
what will get you out of bed in the morning,
what you do with your evenings,
how you spend your weekends,
what you read, whom you know,
what breaks your heart,
and what amazes you with joy and gratitude.

Fall in Love,
stay in love,
and it will decide everything.[1]

---

1. Pedro Arrupe, SJ, "Fall in Love," in *Finding God in All Things:
   A Marquette Prayer Book*, ed. Doug Leonhardt, SJ (Milwaukee:
   Marquette University Press, 2009), 98.

Conclusion

Thank you for accompanying me on my journey, on my pilgrimage to the Mystery in the depths. I hope you have enjoyed the trip and also that you are as intrigued by your own journey as I have been by mine. An examined life is a wonderful thing, a conscious relationship between oneself and one's Creator, a "Holy Communion."

Were you to ask me how I think one ought to live one's life, you probably know what I would say. I would give the same advice I received long ago when, thinking I needed to acquire all the wisdom I could in order to be a priest someday, I opened a philosophy book for the first time and read these words:

Know thyself.

Permissions

Excerpt from "Christian Living Formerly and Today," in *Theological Investigations VII: Further Theology of the Spiritual Life 1*, by Karl Rahner, SJ, trans. David Bourke, copyright © 1971. Permission granted by Darton, Longman & Todd, UK publishers.

Excerpt from "The man who rowed across the ocean" from http://www.ulrich-schaffer.com/Poems.html, a poem by Ulrich Schaffer. Copyright by Ulrich Schaffer. Reprinted by permission. All rights reserved.

Excerpt from "Fall in Love," attributed to Fr. Pedro Arrupe, SJ, from *Finding God in All Things: A Marquette Prayer Book*, Marquette University Press, copyright © 2009. Reprinted by permission. All rights reserved.

Excerpt from *The Red Book* by Carl Jung, W. W. Norton & Company, copyright © 2009. Reprinted with permission. All rights reserved.

Acknowledgements

I am grateful to:

Elyse for her inspiration, understanding, and patience.

Kathryn Stinson, Tom Foley, Linda Austin, and Rick Yakimo for their critiques.

Katherine Pickett, Susan Moore, and Kathy Clayton for copyediting.

Bonnie Spinola for proofreading.

The officers and members of the C.G. Jung Society of Saint Louis for their friendship, wisdom, encouragement, and many educational offerings.

And, the officers and members of the Saint Louis Publishers Association for their expertise, enthusiasm, camaraderie, monthly meetings, and special events. I would have been lost without SLPA, and Peggy Nehmen in particular.